OMAN

Then and Now

Sponsored by

Petroleum Development Oman

His Majesty Sultan Qaboos bin Said

OMAN

Then and Now

by Erik van Scherpenzeel

SPB Academic Publishing bv/The Hague/The Netherlands

Despite all efforts, no contact could be established to obtain copyright permission for the publication of three photographs: Khasab Fort, Seeb Airport and Al Hamra.

ISBN 90 5103 139 4

Schinaafs from the sea, Muskat from the harbour, Muskat harbour from the fishermen's rock, and view of Mutra from the east (1809-1810) by R. Temple, are published by permission of the British Library (X44g).

D'Baaij en de stad Muskette en Materen (The Bay and Towns of Muskette and Materen) (1696) by D. van der Velden is published by permission of the University Library, Leiden (VI-14-7).

Published by SPB Academic Publishing bv, P.O. Box 97747, 2509 GC The Hague, The Netherlands.
Fax:+31 70 330 02 54, E-mail: kugler.spb@wxs.nl.

Graphic design: Cees van Rutten Grafische Vormgeving BNO, The Hague, The Netherlands
Lithography: Oasis Productions, Nieuwerkerk aan den IJssel, The Netherlands
Printed and bound by: Proost n.v., Turnhout, Belgium

CONTENTS

ACKNOWLEDGEMENTS

The author wishes to express his gratitude to all those who helped to make this book possible. Without exception, everyone who was approached made their slides, photographs and other material readily available for publication. I would also like to thank my wife Carla for her patience and support and my brother-in-law, Jurriaan Mastenbroek, who is co-originator of the idea for this book. Special thanks must also go to Petroleum Development Oman LLC (PDO) for their financial and logistical assistance, and in particular to Mansour Al Amry, who coordinated PDO's support and provided advice throughout the project. Finally, I am grateful to S.J. Prakash, who not only took most of the photographs for the NOW theme, but was also a trusted companion on the many journeys we made in Oman.

E. van Scherpenzeel

Contributors to the THEN theme

C. Balhuizen
W. and M. van Beusekom
W.J. van de Bosch
R.A. Bulstra
F.W. Eckenhausen
G.M. Graham
L.W. van Hellemond
J. Horstink
G.J. Mastenbroek
G.L.E. van Meerbeke
E.G.J. van Meerbeke
PDO Archives
W.F. Pilaar
E. van Scherpenzeel
W.F. Steenken
L.J. van Veen
D. van der Wiel

Contributors to the NOW theme

C. van Scherpenzeel
E. van Scherpenzeel
PDO Geomatics Department
Paul Kunert
Gerard Bosman
Rashid Ali Al Hinai
PDO Public Affairs Department
G.R. Greenwell
S.J. Prakash
Al-Zaki Abdulhamid
Saleh Al-Alawi

PREFACE

This book first came into being after I returned from a trip to Oman in 1996. Comparing the photographs that I had just taken with ones that were taken in the late 1960s and early 1970s, I thought that the remarkable changes that have occurred in Oman since July 1970 should really be photographically documented in a book for all to see.

When I began to seriously pursue the project, however, it soon became obvious that a wider selection of pictures was required for a countrywide THEN theme. In the early days, travel restrictions had been in force in some areas, notably Musandam and Dhofar, and the photographic record I had to hand was a bit thin. Consequently, I contacted former colleagues who had worked in Oman many years ago, and they supplied me with more than 5,000 old slides to choose from.

My colleagues' generosity then presented me with the opposite problem: the book's NOW theme was deficient in comparison. With the scope of the book threatening to overwhelm my own modest resources, I approached Petroleum Development Oman for assistance. This was readily given, both financially and logistically. And so, many journeys were made throughout the country to retake the scenes originally captured in the selected THEN photographs.

It had been decided early on that the NOW photographs should not necessarily picture the exact same subject nor be shot from the exact point of view as the corresponding THEN photograph. For one thing, this would often be physically impossible, as in many cases buildings now stand where there was none before. And for another, the photographic comparisons were meant to be impressionistic; they were not intended as a 'spot the difference' game.

It was also not the intention to make this book a nostalgic journey. It is instead an admiring glance at the remarkable progress Oman has undergone since the accession of HM Sultan Qaboos in 1970. Few countries, if any, have been able to undergo a peaceful transformation from an almost medieval situation into a fully equipped modern state - all in the space of 30 years. And what is all the more remarkable is that, in the midst of all this accelerated progress, Oman has managed to retain its rich natural and cultural inheritance.

Erik van Scherpenzeel

FOREWORD *from* HIS EXCELLENCY *the* MINISTER *of* OIL *and* GAS

The Sultanate of Oman is a country with widely contrasting scenery: majestic mountains in the north, lush greenery in the south, shimmering deserts in the west and idyllic coves in the east. But our country's great physical beauty was virtually unknown to the outside world until July 1970, when His Majesty Sultan Qaboos bin Said took over from his father. From thenceforth, Oman underwent a renaissance, transforming itself into a modern state under His Majesty's dynamic leadership.

The remarkable progress Oman has undergone over the last three decades is in large part due to the country's oil and gas industry. Increasing production levels have provided most of the funding for past and present development projects, and growing oil and gas reserves will provide the funding for development projects in the future.

This book reveals - perhaps for the first time to many interested readers - that the success of Oman's oil and gas ventures, now often taken for granted, was preceded by a history of reversals and disappointments. It also shows, through a camera viewfinder, not only our country's many changes since the accession of His Majesty but also its immutabilities: the integrity of its people and the grandeur of its landscapes.

Comparing the "Then" pictures with the "Now" ones, I - for one - am grateful over and over again for His Majesty's unrelenting efforts to improve the welfare of His people and our country.

Dr. Mohammed bin Hamed bin Saif al Rumhy
Minister of Oil and Gas

November 2000

BIBLIOGRAPHY

Beguin Billecocq, Xavier, *Oman: Twenty-Five Centuries of Travel Writing*, Relations Internationales & Culture, Paris, 1994

Van Dam, N. et al., *Nederland en de Arabische wereld van de middeleeuwen tot de twintigste eeuw*, De Tijdstroom, Lochem, 1987

Dinterman, Walter, *Forts of Oman*, Motivate Publishing, 1993

Graham, Gavin, *Oman and PDO-An Introduction*, 1997

Hawley, Sir Donald, *Oman and its Renaissance*, Stacey International, London, 1990

Hill, A. and Hill, D., *The Sultanate of Oman*, Longman, London, 1977

Meyer, Pierre, *Sultanate of Oman*, Editions Delroisse, 1975

Peyton, W.D., *Old Oman*, Stacey International, 1983

Phillips, Wendell, *Oman: A History*, Librairie Du Liban, Beirut, 1971

Skeet, Ian, *Oman Before 1970: The End of an Era*, Faber & Faber, London, 1974

Oman, Department of Information, Muscat, 1972

Oman, A Seafaring Nation, Ministry of National Heritage and Culture, 1979

PDO News-4/1989,-1/1990,- 4/1995,-1,-2/1997,-1/1998

MAJOR MILESTONES *in the* HISTORY *of* OMAN

From as early as 5000 BC, Oman has at various times played a prominent role in the history of both Arabia and the area beyond. The following are some key dates in Oman's history:

Prehistory: Evidence of isolated coastal and inland settlements. Graves at Ras al Hamra dated at 4th millennium BC.

ca. 3000-2000 BC: Oman supplies Dilmun (Bahrein), Mesopotamia and Indus Valley with a range of raw materials including copper. Period of complex burials (Bat tombs near Ibri and Tower tombs in the Eastern Hajar).

ca. 2000-1000 BC: Copper boom declines. Persians occupy Oman and settle along the coast. Arrival of Arab tribes.

ca. 1000-300 BC: Camels domesticated, *falaj* system introduced and rapid growth of agriculture. Cyrus the Great conquers Oman.

300 BC-226 AD: Peak of trading of frankincense from Sumhuram in Dhofar. Azdites tribes under Malik bin Fahm arrive in Oman and defeat Persians.

AD 226-640: Persians regain control of the Batinah coast (Sassanid period). The Al Azd continue to rule the Interior.

630: Conversion of Oman to Islam.

751: Julanda bin Masud elected first Imam.

8th-10th century: Arab trading and seafaring rapidly expands with Sohar as the centre of maritime activities.

1250-1507: Island-state of Hormuz establishes sovereignty over the coast of Oman.

1507-1624: Portuguese under Albuquerque capture Qalhat, Quriyat, Muscat, Sohar and Hormuz, and control trade in the Indian Ocean. Forts Mirani and Jalali in Muscat built.

1624: Nasir bin Murshid, first Imam of the Ya-ruba dynasty elected. Portuguese driven back to Mutrah-Muscat.

1624-1718: Ya-ruba dynasty rules Oman. Portuguese expelled from Oman in 1650. Omani fleet captures Portuguese colonies in East Africa, India and Persia. Building of forts in Nizwa, Jabrin, Rustaq and Hazm.

1718-1747: Civil war between Ghafiri and Hinawi tribes following disagreements on succession of Imam. Persia called in to assist and occupies parts of Oman.

1747: Ahmad bin Said drives the Persians from Oman and is elected first Imam of the Al Bu Said dynasty.

1804-1856: Reign of Sayyid Said bin Sultan Al Bu Said. Golden era of prosperity and expansion for Oman. Seat of government transferred from Muscat to Zanzibar. On the death of Sayyid Said, Oman and Zanzibar are divided into separate sultanates.

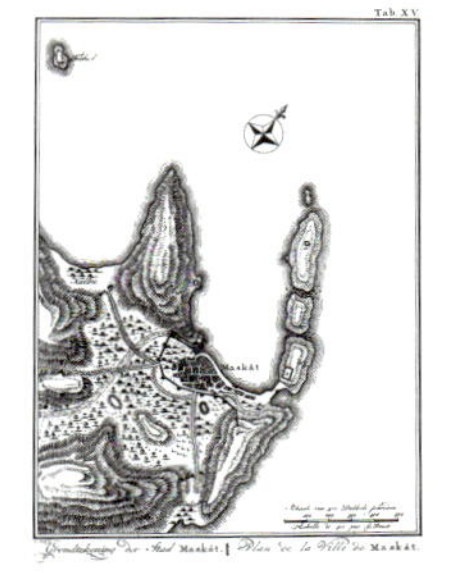

1868-1920: Steady decline of Oman as a maritime power due to opening of the Suez Canal and coming of steam shipping. Period of discord between the Sultan ruling the coastal areas and the Imam controlling the Interior.

1920: Agreement at Seeb between Sultan and Imam on respective spheres of control.

1952-1955: Buraimi conflict among Saudi Arabia, Abu Dhabi and Oman.

1954-1959: Imamate conflict under Ghalib bin Ali, also referred to as the Jebel War.

1965-1975: Communist-led rebellion in Dhofar.

1967: First commercial oil produced in Oman.

1970: Accession of HM Sultan Qaboos bin Said as eighth ruler from the Al Bu Said dynasty.

1970-today: **Oman's Renaissance**. Three decades of large-scale developments in infrastructure, health, education, communication, agriculture, fishing, mining, etc. Oman transformed from an almost medieval country into a modern fully equipped state, taking its rightful place among its neighbours and the rest of the world.

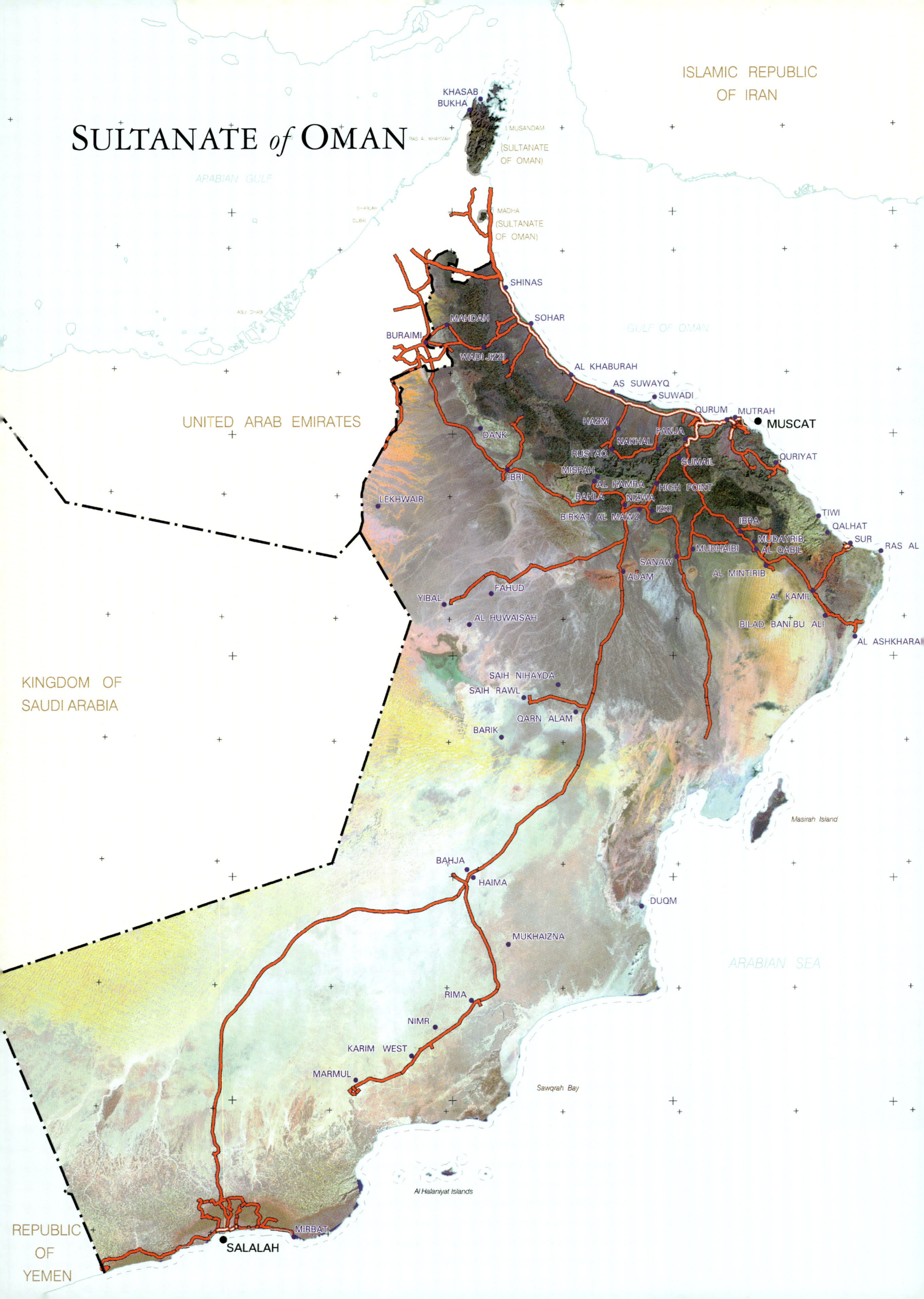

SULTANATE of OMAN
ISLAMIC REPUBLIC OF IRAN
KHASAB
BUKHA
(SULTANATE OF OMAN)
MADHA
(SULTANATE OF OMAN)
SHINAS
SOHAR
MAHDAH
BURAIMI
WADI JIZZI
GULF OF OMAN
AL KHABURAH
AS SUWAYQ
SUWADI
QURUM
MUTRAH
MUSCAT
UNITED ARAB EMIRATES
HAZM
FANJA
NAKHAL
RUSTAQ
DANK
QURIYAT
SUMAIL
MISFAH
IBRI
AL HAMRA
HIGH POINT
BAHLA
NIZWA
LEKHWAIR
IZKI
BIRKAT AL MAWZ
TIWI
IBRA
QALHAT
MUDAYRIB
SUR
AL QABIL
RAS AL
MUDHAIBI
SANAW
ADAM
AL MINTIRIB
FAHUD
YIBAL
AL KAMIL
AL HUWAISAH
BILAD BANI BU ALI
AL ASHKHARA
KINGDOM OF SAUDI ARABIA
SAIH NIHAYDA
SAIH RAWL
QARN ALAM
BARIK
Masirah Island
BAHJA
HAIMA
DUQM
MUKHAIZNA
ARABIAN SEA
RIMA
NIMR
KARIM WEST
MARMUL
Sawqrah Bay
Al Halaniyat Islands
REPUBLIC OF YEMEN
MIRBAT
SALALAH

A Brief History *of the* Oil *and* Gas Industry *in* Oman

Early days (1900-1950)

William Knox D'Arcy, an Englishman who had made his money from gold mining in Australia, discovered the first commercial oil in the Middle East in 1908. His venture became known as the Anglo-Persian Company, subsequently becoming the Anglo-Iranian Oil Company and, later still, The British Petroleum Company (BP). D'Arcy Petroleum, a subsidiary of the seminal Anglo-Persian Company, was the first company to enter Oman with the intention of finding and producing oil.

In 1925 D'Arcy Petroleum was successful in obtaining an exploration licence from Sultan Taimur bin Faisal for a period of two years. During the following winter season, a geological field party, which included George Lees and Washington Gray, left Bait al Falaj with Captain Eccles of the British-Indian army and a group of Muscat levies. Following a route along the beach, the party took a week to reach Al Khaburah. (The trip can now be done by car in two hours.) Subsequently, they followed Wadi Hawasina, traversing gorges 10 to 20 feet wide and vertical walls 40 feet high. To facilitate these crossings, Lees installed a long chain, which is still in place today. After crossing the Oman Mountains, the party proceeded via Wadi Al-Jizi to Sohar, where they arrived on 7 December 1926. Using a boat, they continued further south to Muscat and thereafter via Masirah Island and Duqm to Mirbat in Dhofar.

Lees did a remarkably good job, and his description of the Oman Mountains still captures their essence today:

"The great arc-shaped mountainous belt of Oman, projecting like a spur into the vitals of Persia and with heights reaching 9900 feet, is the most striking feature of the map of Arabia in that it is so obviously abnormal."

Early in 1927 Arnold Wilson, Head of Exploration of D'Arcy Petroleum, said that "...Arabia appeared to be devoid of all prospectivity". As a result, D'Arcy Petroleum allowed its license to lapse and the next few years saw hardly any activity in the area.

In 1937 Petroleum Concessions Ltd., a subsidiary of the Iraq Petroleum Company (IPC), signed an agreement under which an option was granted to take up a concession lasting 75 years for the territories of Oman and Dhofar. The exploration and production operations were to be run by Petroleum Development (Oman and Dhofar) Ltd. The operating company had four shareholders, each with an interest of 23.75%: Shell, Anglo-Persian, Compagnie Française des Pétroles (whose convoluted lineage would make it a predecessor of today's TotalFina-Elf) and the Near East Development Company (whose likewise convoluted lineage would make it a predecessor of today's ExxonMobil). The remaining 5% stake was held by a fifth shareholder, Partex.

IPC geologists carried out coastal fieldwork in 1937-1938 from a base in Dubai. However, a more extensive survey programme planned for the Interior during 1938-1939 ended in failure since, despite Government assurances, the personnel became the target of gunfire as soon as they left Sohar. Meanwhile, commercial oil had been discovered in Bahrain in 1932, and in Kuwait and Saudi Arabia in 1938. These discoveries called for a re-focus of activities in Oman.

Apart from some aerial surveys, all fieldwork in Oman was suspended during World War II. However, in 1944 the earlier option agreements were converted into full concessions. After the war, activities remained low key because of tribal unrest. Following brief geological investigations in 1948, the company indicated its intention to relinquish the Dhofar concession. The relinquishment was approved in January 1951 and, consequently, the company changed its name to Petroleum Development (Oman) Ltd.

Fig. 1. Looking down on the drilling of Fahud-1 in 1956.

North Oman (1951-1960)

In the early 1950s, after sighting a large surface anticline from the air, geologists became very interested in the Fahud area. The rock formation appeared to be very similar to the Jebel Dukhan formation in Qatar, where oil had recently been found.

In 1954 Sultan Said agreed that the company could enter the Interior via the Huqf area in the south. So, in early October 1954 a field party, escorted by a strong military force, set out. Progress through Wadi Musallim and Fahud was slower than expected because of the continuing civil unrest. But the Sultan's forces were able to restore order, actually retaking Ibri and Nizwa, which had fallen into the hands of anti-Government elements.

The company then carried out further fieldwork and properly established itself in Oman. A rig was transported in sections by RAF transport planes from Qatar to Fahud, and the first road was built between Fahud and Izki. The drilling of Well Fahud-1 began on 18 January 1956. The company had such high hopes for the well that a film crew was flown in to record the testing of the well - the first ever

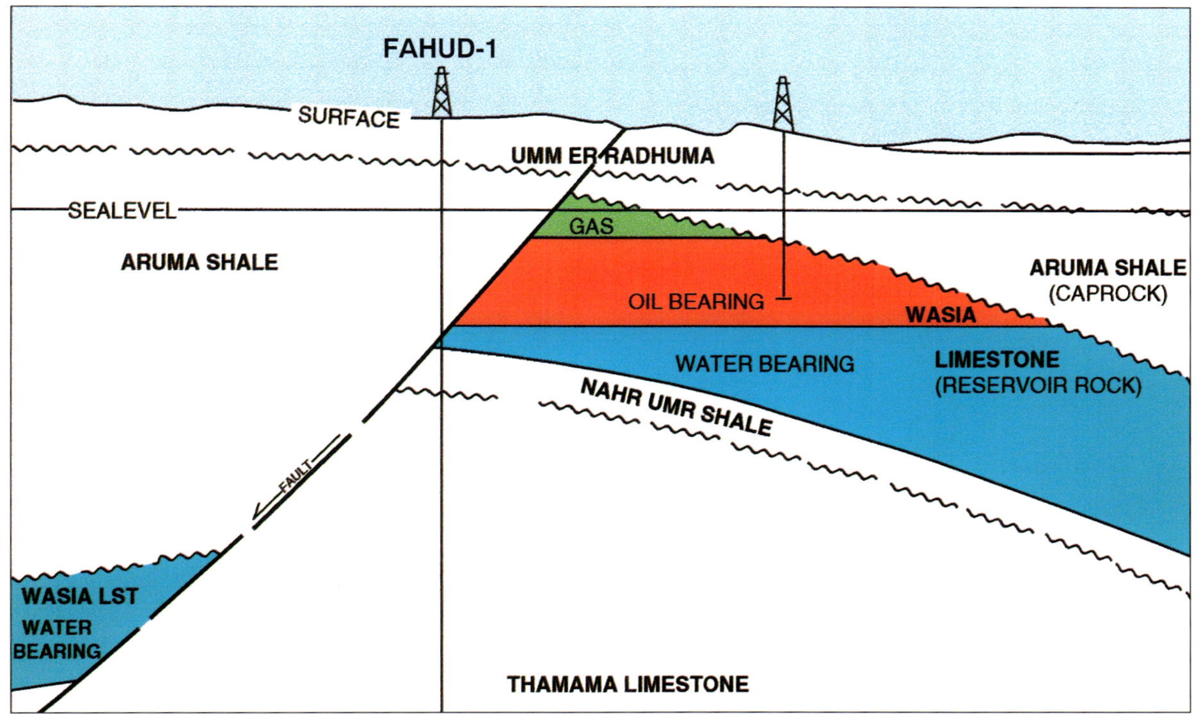

Fig. 2. Cross-section of the Fahud structure, showing how the first well just missed the oil reservoir.

in Oman. After reaching a depth of 3000 metres, however, Fahud-1 was abandoned as a dry hole on 28 May 1957 *(Fig. 1)*. What no-one knew at the time was that the well had missed a multibillion-barrel oilfield by just a few hundred meters *(Fig. 2)*. Not surprisingly, Fahud-1 is often described as the unluckiest well in the history of oil in the Middle East.

Meanwhile, PD(O) had moved its base from Duqm to Azaiba on the Batinah coast. Continuing unrest, however, hampered its activities; from time to time landmines were laid in the Sumail Gap in the mountains. Nevertheless, the company managed to drill two exploration wells during the Jebel War, Ghaba-1 in 1959 and Haima-1 in 1960. These wells, both conclusively dry, were followed later in 1960 by Afar-1, a relatively shallow well, which proved to be equally disappointing.

Having spent more than $ 12 million without any success, and facing significant additional expenditure and logistical problems related to the acquisition of new rigs as well as new seismic and gravimetric data, IPC decided to relinquish its concession in Oman. Shell and Partex, however, opted to continue, while the remaining partners - the Compagnie Française des Pétroles, BP (which had by then succeeded Anglo-Persian) and the Near East Development Company - pulled out.

Dhofar (1951-1966)

Following the relinquishment of the Dhofar concession, in January 1951 Sultan Said awarded the acreage to Wendell Phillips, an American archaeologist who had carried out excavations near Sohar. He was then working in Dhofar, where he had discovered the remains of the city of Sumhuram, an ancient frankincense port.

Phillips subsequently managed to farm out the concession to the newly formed Dhofar-Cities Service Petroleum Corporation, a 50/50 joint venture between Cities Service and the Richfield Corporation of California. Through his Philpryor Corporation, Phillips kept a 2.5% overriding royalty.

Exploration activities started in 1953 and, after three disappointing wells, the Marmul oil field - a classical anticlinal feature - was discovered in 1957 *(Fig. 3)*.

Fig. 3. Plaque erected by Dhofar-Cities Service following the discovery of oil at Marmul in 1956. This find was initially thought to be uneconomic.

Fig. 4. Well Yibal-1 in 1962. The wali *of Ibri is present at the start of drilling.*

However, subsequent appraisal drilling failed to establish sustainable oil production rates. By the end of 1961 Dhofar-Cities Service had drilled 23 wells, including six with a depth of over 3000 metres, and had spent some $ 35 million - but had very little to show for it. As a consequence, Richfield withdrew from the venture. (Ironically, subsequent evaluations in the late 1970s showed Marmul to be one of the larger Omani oil fields.)

In 1962 Cities Service entered into an agreement with John Mecom, one of the leading Texas independents, and the Pure Oil Company; Philpryor still retained its 2.5% overriding royalty. By early 1965 Mecom and Pure Oil had drilled five more wells, but again with disappointing results. At this point, the Continental Oil Company joined the Dhofar concession with a one-third interest; one-third remained with Mecom, while Union Oil Company of California took over Pure Oil's one-third share. One well, Montassar-1, located at the edge of the Rub al Khali, was drilled in 1966 with negative results. In view of the civil unrest in Dhofar and the lack of success, Continental Oil and its partners finally surrendered the Dhofar concession.

Commercial oil (1961-1969)

Following the withdrawal of three of the original five partners, the shareholding of Petroleum Development (Oman) was split between Shell (85%) and Partex (15%). No further drilling took place until 1962, after seismic surveys had confirmed the geological structure that gravimetric surveys had first identified at Yibal. But Well Yibal-1, whose drilling began on 28 May 1962 *(Fig. 4)*, encountered technical problems. The drilling rig was therefore moved nearby so that another well could be sunk. The drilling of Yibal-2 began in June 1962. On entering the Natih formation, the well unexpectedly encountered large amounts of natural gas, resulting in a blow out. Fortunately, nobody was hurt. Drilling was resumed and, on 11 September 1962, a light crude oil was found in the Shuaiba formation.

On 5 April 1963 the rig was moved to the Natih area to test a surface anticline, similar to but smaller than Fahud. Well Natih-1 proved to be successful and was quickly followed up by Natih-2 and Natih-3. The stratigraphic information provided by the Yibal and Natih

Figs. 5 and 6. Laying the main Fahud-Saih Al Maleh (MAF) pipeline in 1966.

Fig. 7. Highest point of the main pipeline at the Izki watershed (650 m).

Fig. 8. Construction of the main crude tank farm at Saih Al Maleh (MAF).

wells shed new light on the seven-year-old results of Well Fahud-1, encouraging PD(O) to try again at Fahud. And so the drilling of Well Fahud-2 began on 5 February 1964. Located a kilometre and a half from Fahud-1, the new well proved that the whole Natih formation contained oil. As such, it can be viewed as a major discovery. Based on a presumed leak to the press, a report on the oil successes in Oman appeared in the London *Sunday Times* of 26 July 1964. The 'official' announcement of commercial oil followed on 2 November 1964.

Investment in a pipeline to the coast and in all the other hardware necessary for the transport and export of Oman's crude was now started, and plans were made for the first export. In addition, exploration continued with renewed confidence and vigour.

The development of the fields and production

Fig. 9. Loading the Mosprince with the first oil cargo from Oman in 1967.

facilities at Fahud, including a 20-megawatt power plant, ran apace. And plans for the processing, storing and shipping complex at Saih al-Maleh (later re-named Mina al-Fahal) on the coast were prepared. Linking one site with the other would be a pipeline 276 kilometres long and, at its highest point at the Izki watershed, some 650 metres above sea level. It was a massive engineering challenge and a politically complex task.

Work started in March 1966. To complete the pipeline, a total of 60,000 tons of steel pipes were imported, transported and laid, and associated pumping facilities and other hardware installed. The labour for these tasks was provided by the villages encountered along the way *(Figs. 5, 6, 7 and 8)*. The entire development - including a chain of radio repeater stations, the industrial area and tank farm at Saih al-Maleh, the housing for staff near the industrial area, and the pipeline to the coast - cost a total of $ 70 million.

The first export of Omani oil, loaded onto the tanker Mosprince at Saih al-Maleh, took place on 27 July 1967. The original debit note shows that the consignment consisted of 543,800 barrels of Omani crude valued at $1.42 a barrel *(Figs. 9 and 10)*.

With its first shipment of crude oil, Oman entered a new age. In the wake of the exploration successes, extensive geological studies of the Oman Mountains, including two large field surveys, were carried out during the period 1966-1969 under the leadership of K.W. Glennie. These studies greatly contributed to the current understanding of the geological history of the Oman Mountains. It is interesting to note that the conclusions of these studies in essence confirmed the work done by Lees 40 years earlier.

In the meantime, in June 1967, the Compagnie Française des Pétroles rejoined the partnership by taking over two-thirds of Partex's equity share, resulting in the following shareholding: Shell 85%, Compagnie Francaise des Petroles 10% and Partex 5%. In 1969 the partnership regained the Dhofar concession under an agreement similar in terms to the revised agreement made in the north of the country in 1967. By 1974, the Dhofar concession was fully integrated into the main concession.

Fig. 10. Three stamps commemorating the first shipment of oil in 1967.

Fig. 11. The first visit of HM Sultan Qaboos to the PD(O) offices on 18 August, 1970.

Fig. 12. HM Sultan Qaboos inspects the Oil Installation Police during his visit to the PD(O) offices.

Expansion of oil industry (1970-2000)

On 23 July 1970, His Majesty Sultan Qaboos took over from his father as ruler of the country. He made his first visit to the PD(O) offices on 18 August 1970 *(Figs. 11 and 12)*.

Meanwhile, at the coast, the newly installed 900,000-barrel crude-oil storage tank became operational, allowing crude to be loaded onto moored tankers at a rate of 56,000 barrels/hour. Also in 1970 Oman's share of the profits was raised from 50% to 55%.

A fascinating aspect of the exploration history of Oman has been the perpetuation of its petroleum reserves. Whenever an established oil field appeared to be past its prime, creative thinking, technology and serendipity either revealed a new oil-bearing rock formation that could be exploited or gave the established field a new lease of life by increasing its recoverable reserves. So, while the heavy viscous crude oil first encountered in the Haushi formation of the Marmul field in 1957 was originally thought to be uneconomic to produce, in 1972 the Ghaba North discovery definitely established the true commercial nature of such heavy-oil fields. That realisation was followed up by significant discoveries in Saih Nihayda and Saih Rawl in 1972 and 1973, respectively. These fields, plus the 1971-1972 Qarn Alam and Habur discoveries, are all located in the Ghaba area *(Fig. 13)*. All five fields - Ghaba North, Saih Nihayda, Saih Rawl, Qarn Alam and Habur - were on stream by 1975, the oil being transported via a new 20-inch pipeline that joined the main pipeline 75 kilometres east of Fahud. As a result, production was increased to 340,000 barrels/day.

On 1 January 1974 the Oman Government acquired a 25% shareholding in the PD(O) concession, which was increased to 60% in July 1974, backdated to the beginning of the year *(Fig. 14)*. As a result, the foreign partnership was now made up of Shell (34%), Compagnie Française des Pétroles (4%) and Partex (2%).

The oil price hike of 1973 greatly improved the economics of oil in south Oman and, as a consequence, the focus of exploration activity was moved to the eastern flank of the south Oman salt basin during the 1970s. Initial campaigns discovered the Amal and Amin fields, among others. These discoveries were followed by a string of others

Fig. 13. The Saih Nihaydah field, one of five fields in the Ghaba area brought on stream in 1975.

Fig. 14. HM Sultan Qaboos signs the participation agreement whereby the Government acquired a 25% holding in PDO on 1 January 1974. In July of that year, the holding increased to 60%.

in the Haushi formation during the late 1970s and early 1980s. The Rahab, Nimr and Rima fields *(Fig. 15)*, and discoveries at Suwaihat and Sayyala in central Oman, established beyond doubt the existence of commercial hydrocarbons in regions of the country other than in the north. A development plan was then drawn up to route the pipeline northwards to Qarn Alam. All fields en route were to be hooked up to the pipeline, providing the opportunity for a good mixing of light and heavy crude types. Some $ 350 million was spent on this project, including the construction of the production facilities and the Marmul camp *(Figs. 16 and 17)*.

On 15 November 1980, as part of Oman's tenth National Day celebrations, production commenced in the south *(Fig. 18)*. (Six months earlier, on 15 May 1980, Petroleum Development Oman - now without parentheses in its name - had been registered by Royal Decree as a limited liability company.) In 1981 PDO was producing 320,000 barrels/day, of which 50,000 barrels/day came from the south. In 1982 a refinery with a capacity of 50,000 barrels/day was opened in Mina al-Fahal to secure a domestic supply of petroleum products.

Since the early 1980s, total production at PDO has been steadily increasing - from 500,000 barrels/day in 1985 to 600,000 barrels/day in 1988, 800,000 barrels/day in 1995 and some 832,000 barrels/day in 1999, of which the south contributed almost half.

Some of this increase has arisen from the application of the latest technology to increase oil recovery in existing fields. Such technological means have included steam injection (to thin the heavy oil so that it flows more freely), horizontal and multi-branched wells (to collect the oil flowing through rock layers more efficiently), and computer-based models (to predict the underground flow of the oil more accurately).

Fig. 15. Rima camp in south Oman opened in 1982.

Figs. 16 and 17. The Marmul field, which started production in 1982.

The balance of the production increase over the years has been made up of "new oil" from fields that have not only been found but also developed at an accelerating pace. During the period 1967-1980 all of PDO's production came from 11 fields; by 1988, 50 fields provided the sum total of PDO's oil output; by 1990 this was 60, and in 1999 it was nearly 100 *(Fig. 23)* - including the large, heavy-oil Mukhaizna field.

To meet its highly ambitious double goal of increasing production while also increasing reserves, PDO will have to rely on the continued success of both its exploration and petroleum engineering activities, while at the same time improving its cost base.

Gas development (1978-2000)

Although the PDO concession agreement only covered the development and production of oil and any associated gas, a 345-kilometre, 20-inch gas pipeline was constructed in 1978 on behalf of the Government, to bring non-associated gas from the Yibal field to Al Ghubra on the coast. There, it would be used to generate electricity and to fuel a new desalination plant *(Figs. 19 and 20)*. In 1981 the gas line was extended via a 230-kilometre, 16-inch pipeline along the Batinah coast to Sohar, to provide power for copper mining operations. At the same time, plants for the extraction of liquids from the associated gas were constructed in Yibal, Fahud and Saih Rawl, thereby converting into a saleable product the gas that would otherwise have been flared. In addition, in 1980 another plant was opened at Yibal to produce propane (for PDO cooling systems) and butane (for a bottling plant at Rusail).

In 1984 a further agreement was signed, whereby PDO would search for gas on behalf of the Government. Increases in the gas reserves, if large enough, could justify the exportation of gas, thereby supplementing Oman's oil income. This policy soon proved to be highly successful, with major discoveries in the sandstones of the deep Haima group, notably at Saih Nihayda, Saih Rawl and Barik in the Ghaba salt basin. By the early 1990s, non-associated gas reserves had trebled, amply meeting the forecasted requirements for domestic demand, and providing sufficient gas volumes for a liquefied natural gas (LNG) export scheme. In August 1996 an LNG project, involving the transport of gas through a 353-kilometre, 48-inch pipeline from a processing plant at Saih Rawl in central Oman to a liquefaction plant at Sur on the coast, was approved.

The Oman LNG (OLNG) scheme is by far the largest single project the country has ever undertaken, requiring huge investments both to find, produce and pipe the gas and to treat, liquefy and ship it. PDO commissioned the upstream end of the project, including the gas fields, the processing plant at Saih Rawl and the pipeline to the OLNG plant, during the fourth quarter of 1999 *(Figs. 21 and 22)*. The first ship-borne exports from OLNG took place in 2000, with Korea being the principal customer.

Fig. 18. HE Said bin Ahmed Al Shanfari starts up the southern Oman fields in November 1980.

Economic impact

The discovery of oil in the Middle East has had a huge impact on the economies and way of life of all countries in the region, and Oman is no exception. Oil revenues have to a large extent been responsible for financing the multitude of developments Oman has witnessed on all fronts since 1970.

The oil income of the Sultanate comprises revenues generated by the Government's 60% shareholding in PDO, as well as the taxes and royalties imposed on the foreign companies holding the other 40% interest in the company. With its production target, as of the year 2000, standing at 850,000 barrels/day, the oil sector provides a large percentage of Oman's national income.

Yet Oman's hydrocarbon reserves are modest in comparison to those of other countries in the Gulf area. For that reason diversification has been a very important element in the Sultanate's economic planning. And a major new contributor to the national coffers will be the LNG project that resulted from the dedicated gas-exploration campaign initiated by the Government in the 1980s.

Fig. 19. HM Sultan Qaboos opens the Yibal gas plant in 1978.

Fig. 20. View of the Yibal gas plant.

Fig. 21. On the occasion of the official opening of the Saih Rawl gas plant, HH Sayyid Thuwaini bin Shihab is presented with a commerative gift (1 December 1999).

Fig. 22. The Oman LNG plant near Sur.

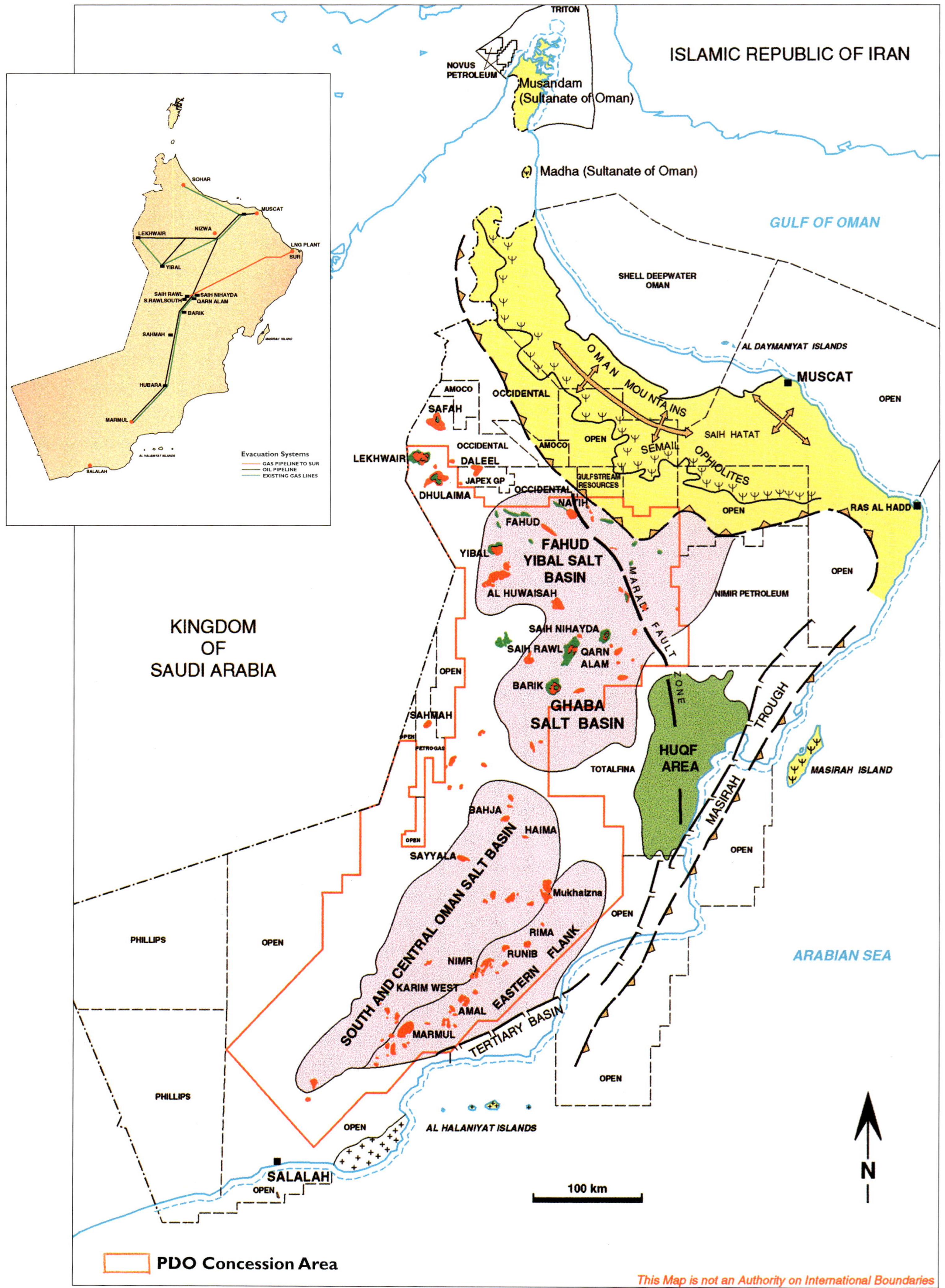

Figs. 23a and b. Occurrence of oil and gas in Oman, and Oman evacuation systems.

Oman, detail from map of Arabia (Tallis 1851) عمان على خارطة شبه الجزيرة العربية (تاليس ١٨٥١)

Prehistoric rock engravings of camels at Tawi (Musandam)

نقوش صخرية لجمال في قرية طوي (مسندم) تعود إلى ما قبل التاريخ

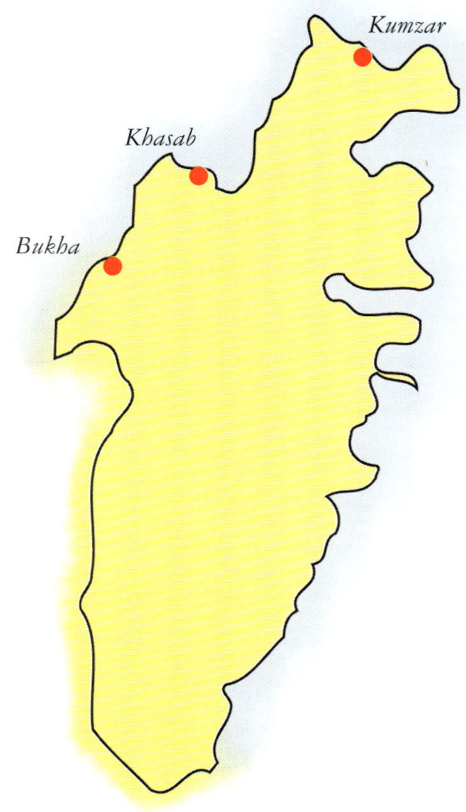

Musandam

MUSANDAM, the smallest and most northerly province of Oman, is separated from the rest of the country by a 70-kilometre stretch of the UAE. It covers the area where the Hajar mountain range plunges dramatically into the Arabian Gulf. Musandam has always been strategically very important since it controls the entrance to the Arabian Gulf through the Straits of Hormuz, one of the busiest shipping lanes in the world.

The Musandam peninsula comprises a massive limestone plateau with an average height of some 800 m, and has a coastline characterised by towering cliffs and numerous deep rocky inlets, giving it a "fjord-like" appearance. The main villages of this thinly populated province, i.e., Khasab, Bukha and Kumzar, are all located on the coast and are built where a *wadi* opens up to the sea. With fresh water being very scarce and little land being available for cultivation, the sea is strongly relied on for food, trade and communications. Khasab is the capital of Musandam.

الخط الساحلي المتعرج لمسندم جعلها
تبدو وكأنها جرف بحري ، ٢٠٠٠

Musandam's convoluted coastline, giving it a "fjord-like" appearance, 2000.

مسندم التي يعمل سكانها في مهنة الصيد
ترقد على سفح منحدرات شاهقة من
الحجر الجيري، ٢٠٠٠

Musandam, fishing village nestling at the foot of towering limestone cliffs, 2000.

خور نجد بمسندم،
٢٠٠٠

Musandam, Khawr Najd fjord, 2000.

طفلات من مسندم، ١٩٨٢

Musandam, girls, 1982.

مسندم، شاب يحمل الجرز التقليدي
وهو عبارة عن رأس فاس صغيرة
مثبت فوق عصا طويلة، ١٩٨٢

Musandam, young man with the traditional jerz, *a small axehead on a long handle, 1982.*

BUKHA is located 25 kilometres west of Khasab along a wide crescent-shaped bay ringed by mountains. There are two forts, one of which is in ruins.

مسندم، منظر لقرية بخا من الجنوب وتبدو
قلعة البلاد في الوسط، ١٩٨٢

Musandam, view of Bukha village from the south with Al Bilad fort in the centre, 1982.

منظر لبخا من
القلعة، ١٩٨٢

Bukha, outlook from hilltop fort, 1982.

قلعة البلاد في بخا التي تم بناؤها في
القرن السابع عشر مع برج المراقبة
الذي يتخذ شكل الكمثرى، ١٩٨٢

Bukha, 17th century Al Bilad fort with its pear-shaped watchtower, 1982.

تقع بخاء على بعد ٢٥ كيلومترا غربي خصب على طول خليج واسع شبه دائري تحف به الجبال. وتوجد بها قلعتان إحداهما لم تبق منها إلا أطلال .

مسندم، منظر لبخا من الجنوب، ٢٠٠٠

Musandam, view of Bukha from the south, 2000.

بخا، قلعة البلاد وشارع الكورنيش، ٢٠٠٠

Bukha, Al Bilad fort and corniche, 2000.

بخا منظر من القلعة، ٢٠٠٠

Bukha, outlook from hilltop fort, 2000.

Khasab, the main coastal town, has a natural harbour with high cliffs on both sides. Centred around an old Portuguese fort, it has some 5000 inhabitants, corresponding to approximately half the total population of Musandam. Traditionally, agriculture (date farming) and fishing are the main occupations. But nowadays import-export shops abound in the town, and there is daily trade in and around the harbour, notably with Iran and the UAE.

Khasab, wali *and sheikhs gathered in front of the fort, 1976.* خصب، الوالي والشيوخ أمام القلعة، ١٩٧٦

ميناء خصب، ١٩٨٢

Khasab harbour, 1982.

فندق خصب، ١٩٨٣

Khasab Hotel, 1983.

خصب هي المدينة الساحلية الرئيسية وبها مرفأ طبيعي تحف به الجبال الشاهقة من كل جانب وتوجد في وسط المدينة قلعة برتغالية قديمة . ويبلغ عدد سكان المدينة نحو ٥٠٠٠ نسمة وهم يشكلون تقريبا نصف سكان شبه جزيرة مسندم وظلت الزراعة (النخيل) وصيد الأسماك منذ القدم تمثل مصدر الرزق الرئيسي إلا أن المحلات التجارية التي تعمل في الاستيراد والتصدير تنتشر الآن في المدينة ويشهد المرفأ حركة تجارية يومية وبخاصة مع إيران ودولة الإمارات العربية المتحدة .

قلعة خصب، ٢٠٠٠

Khasab fort, 2000.

ميناء خصب، ٢٠٠٠

Khasab harbour, 2000.

فندق خصب، ٢٠٠٠

Khasab Hotel, 2000.

Kumzar, a small fishing village, lies tucked away at the northernmost tip of Musandam and is only accessible by boat. Typical of the area are the elaborately decorated bows and sterns of the fishing dhows *(battils)*, a few of which can still be seen today.

قرية كمزار، ٢٠٠٠

Kumzar village, 2000.

كمزاري يدخن الشيشة، ٢٠٠٠

Kumzar, enjoying a waterpipe, 2000.

قوارب البتيل وقد زينت مقدمتها ومؤخرتها بجلود الماعز وعقود مشبوكة من القواقع والأساور والأشرطة الملونة

Kumzari battils *with their bows and sterns decorated with goat skins, ribbons and cowrie shells, 2000.*

تحتل قرية كمزار أقصى الطرف الشمالي من شبه الجزيرة ولا يمكن الوصول إليها إلا عن طريق البحر .و تتميز القرية بالمراكب الصغيرة التقليدية (البتيل) التى أتقن تزيين مقدمتها ومؤخرتها والتي ما زالت تشاهد إلى يومنا هذا .

Musandam, the remains of a fort set against a background of majestic limestone mountains, 2000.

أطلال قلعة أمام جبل مهيب من الحجر الجيري، ٢٠٠٠

Musandam, Acacia woodland at Birkat Khaldiyah, 2000.

مسندم أشجار الصمغ العربي في بركة خلدياب، ٢٠٠٠

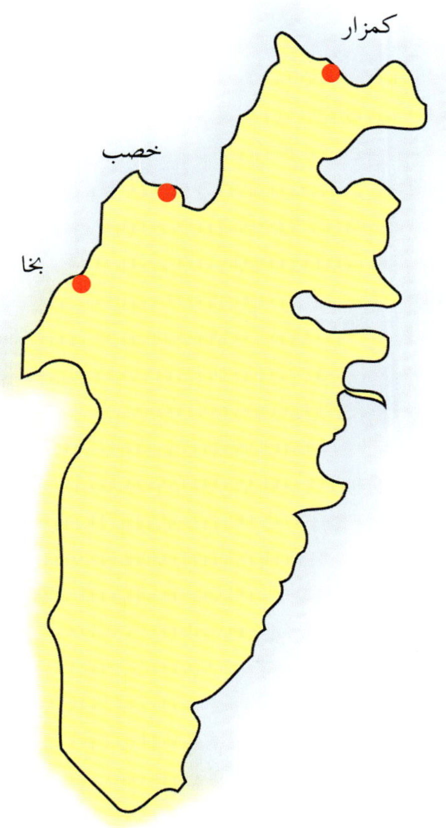

مسندم

تعد مسندم أصغر محافظة في السلطنة وتقع في أقصى الطرف الشمالي ويفصلها عن بقية أجزاء السلطنة شريط يمتد بمسافة ٧٠ كيلومترا عن أراضي دولة الإمارات العربية المتحدة . وتغطي المنطقة التي تنحدر فيها سلسلة جبال الحجر بشدة في الخليج العربي. وظلت مسندم دائما تتمتع بأهمية استراتيجية بالغة بحكم سيطرتها على الممر المائي المؤدي إلى الخليج العربي عبر مضيق هرمز وهو أحد أكثر خطوط الملاحة البحرية العالمية حركة . وتتكون شبه جزيرة مسندم من هضبة جيرية ضخمة يبلغ متوسط ارتفاعها نحو ٨٠٠ مترا وتحد خط ساحلها جبال شاهقة والعديد من المنافذ الصحراوية العميقة مما يجعلها تبدو وكأنها "جرف بحري". وشبه جزيرة مسندم ليست كثيفة السكان وتقع قراها الرئيسية وهي خصب وبخاء وكمزار – على الساحل وكلها مشيدة في واد يتجه صوب البحر. ونظرا لقلة المياه العذبة وندرة الأراضي الزراعية يعتمد سكان مسندم بشكل رئيسي على البحر في معيشتهم وتجارتهم وتنقلهم . وخصب هي عاصمة محافظة مسندم .

Alfonso d'Albuquerque at Maskate (1507). الفونس ألبوكيرك في مسقط (١٥٠٧)

View of Muscat Harbour (Olfert Dapper 1680)

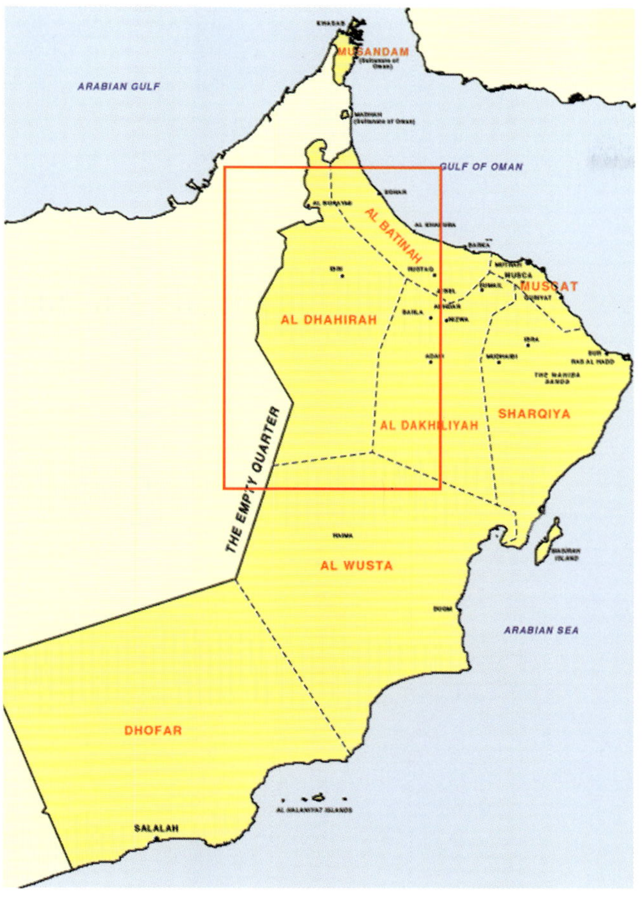

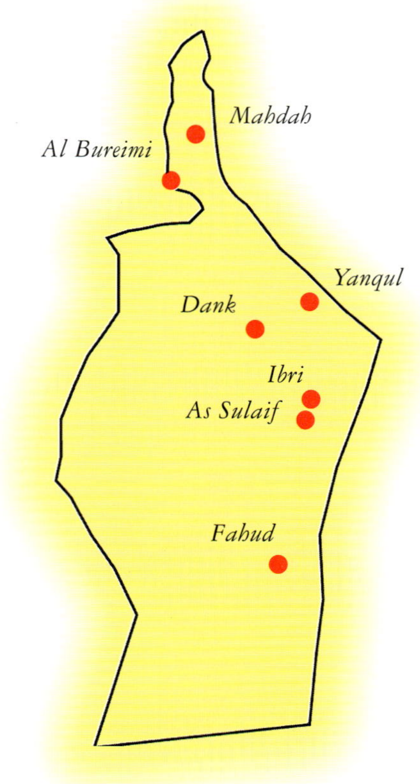

Al Dhahirah

The Dhahirah province, comprising the northwest shoulder of Oman, is wedged between the western Hajar Mountains and the Empty Quarter. It extends from Mahdah in the north via Bureimi and Ibri to Fahud in the south, and is largely made up of desert terrain. The principal town of the Dhahirah is Ibri, some 100 kilometres west of Bahla. The Dhahirah is linked to the Batinah coast by two routes: the *wadi* Jizzi from Bureimi to Sohar, and the *wadi* Hawasina from Ibri to Al Khaboura.

The Dhahirah area is the heartland of the Duru tribe, one of the four main Beduin tribes in Oman. Tanam, near Ibri, is their capital. The Duru occupy a very large area, with their main activities of herding camels, goats and sheep, centred around the *wadi*s Al Ayn, Aswad and Amairi. As the first major oil discoveries - the Fahud, Yibal and Natih fields - are located in their land, the Duru have benefited more than most from the oil, particularly in terms of employment. Efforts to resettle the Duru and other Beduin into new housing areas are being actively pursued by the government, but some still opt for a truly nomadic lifestyle.

Dhahira, camel caravan near Ibri, 1972.

الظاهرة، قافلة من الجمال قرب عبري، ١٩٧٢

Dhahirah, Duru women and children, 1967. الظاهرة، امرأة وأطفال من قبيلة الدروع، ١٩٦٧

الظاهرة، رجل من الدروع أمام خيمته، ١٩٩٨

Dhahirah, Duru man in front of his shelter, 1998.

الظاهرة، طفلة من الدروع، ١٩٦٧

Dhahirah, Duru girl, 1967.

Situated next to a series of low hills amid a sea of date palms, Ibri is strategically placed to control the *wadi* Hawasina route to the coast and the interior route to Nizwa. While Bureimi has been described as the gateway to Oman, Ibri is considered to be the inner door, i.e., whoever controls Ibri has relatively easy access to Nizwa.

منظر لمدينة عبري
وواحتها، ١٩٦٦

View of the town of Ibri and its oasis, 1966.

ساحة سوق عبري أمام
القلعة، ١٩٦٦

Ibri market square in front of the fort, 1966.

تقع عبري خلف سلسلة من التلال المنخفضة ووسط كم هائل من أشجار النخيل وتحتل موقعا استراتيجيا يمكنها من التحكم على طريق وادي الحواسنة المتجه إلى الساحل وعلى طريق الداخلية المؤدي إلى نزوى. فإذا كانت البريمي قد وصفت بأنها بوابة عمان فإن عبري هي الباب الداخلي بمعنى أن من كان يتحكم على عبري فمن السهل عليه نسبيا الوصول إلى نزوى .

منظر لمدينة عبري وسط أشجار النخيل، ٢٠٠٠

View of Ibri town amid the vast date plantations, 2000.

ساحة سوق عبري وتبدو في الخلف قلعة عبري التي تم ترميمها، ٢٠٠٠

Ibri market square with the renovated fort in the background, 2000.

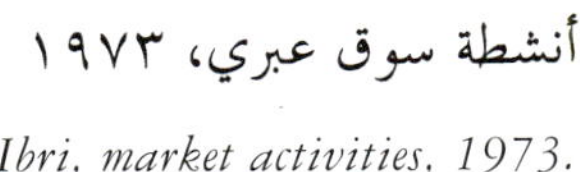

أنشطة سوق عبري، ١٩٧٣

Ibri, market activities, 1973.

تجمع الجمهور أمام قلعة عبري استعداداً للاحتفال بعيد الأضحى المبارك، ١٩٦٢

Ibri, crowd gathering in front of the fort on the occasion of the Eid Al Adha festivities, 1962.

Ibri, entrance to the suq, 1964.

مدخل سوق عبري، ١٩٦٤

بيع الفواكه في سوق عبري، ٢٠٠٠
Ibri market, fruit seller, 2000.

سوق عبري، ٢٠٠٠
Ibri market, 2000.

سوق الماشية في عبري أمام القلعة، ٢٠٠٠
Ibri goat market in front of the fort, 2000.

Ibri, entrance to the suq, 2000.
مدخل سوق عبري، ٢٠٠٠

سوق عبري، ١٩٧٢
Ibri suq, 1972.

خياط يمارس عمله في سوق عبري، ١٩٧٢
Ibri suq, tailor at work, 1972.

Ibri suq, 1972. سوق عبري، ١٩٧٢

سوق عبري، ٢٠٠٠ *Ibri suq, 2000.*

متجر عام في سوق عبري، ٢٠٠٠
Ibri suq, general store, 2000.

خنجر للبيع في سوق عبري، ٢٠٠٠
Ibri suq, khanjars *for sale, 2000.*

محل خياطة ملابس نسائية بعبري، ٢٠٠٠
Ibri suq, ladies dressmaker, 2000.

واحة عبري، ١٩٦٢

Ibri oasis, 1962.

مقهى ومطعم، ١٩٦٦

Ibri, National Hotel, 1966.

فتاة تحمل دلو ماء فوق رأسها، ١٩٧٢

Ibri, girl carrying water, 1972.

منظر من خلال إحدى
بوابات المدينة القديمة
لواحة عبري، ٢٠٠٠

Ibri oasis, view through one of the old city gates, 2000.

فندق عبري، ٢٠٠٠

Ibri Hotel, 2000.

نقطة تعبئة ناقلات توزيع المياه،
٢٠٠٠

Ibri, water tanks filling up for further distribution, 2000.

Al Sulaif, a small fortified village a few kilometres east of Ibri, is built on a prominent rock at the edge of the *wadi* Al Ayn. It was deserted many years ago when the *falaj* dried up and most of the original town is now in ruins. Recently, a few new houses have been built along the banks of the *wadi*.

Al Sulaif when it was still inhabited.
View from the wadi *Al Ayn, 1961.*

السليف عندما كانت مأهولة
منظر من وادي العين، ١٩٦١

Al Sulaif, view from the east, 1961.

منظر للسليف من الشرق، ١٩٦١

السليف قرية صغيرة محصنة تقع على بعد بضعة كيلومترات شرقي عبري وبنيت فوق صخرة كبيرة في نهاية وادي العين. وقد هجرها سكانها قبل عدة سنوات حين جف الفلج وقد أصبحت اجزاء كثيرة من المدينة الأصلية أطلالا الآن . وشيدت مؤخرا بعض المساكن على ضفتي الوادي .

منظر للسليف من وادي العين، ٢٠٠٠

Al Sulaif, view from the wadi *Al Ayn, 2000.*

كتابة محفورة قرب بوابة الدخول إلى السليف، ٢٠٠٠

Al Sulaif, inscription next to the entrance gate, 2000.

Al Sulaif, view from the east, 2000. منظر للسليف من الشرق، ٢٠٠٠

Dariz, sheikh with his askaris*, 1967.*
شيخ من الدريز مع عسكره، ١٩٦٧

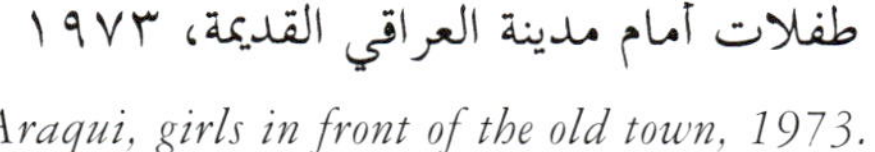

طفلات أمام مدينة العراقي القديمة، ١٩٧٣
Araqui, girls in front of the old town, 1973.

امرأة في سوق عبري، ٢٠٠٠
Ibri, woman at the market, 2000.

Ibri, young man, 1962. شاب من عبري، ١٩٦٢

شيوخ من العراقي، ١٩٧٣
Old men at Araqui, 1973.

شيخ من عبري، ١٩٦٢
Ibri, old man, 1962.

The Bureimi oasis straddles the border of Oman and the UAE and is strategically situated for access to the Batinah coast via the *wadi* Jizzi, to Ibri-Nizwa and to the UAE.

Over the past 30 years, Bureimi has been transformed into a new and sprawling town with its full complement of modern facilities, but tucked away in the vast date groves, some authentic, traditional village dwellings still remain.

مدخل قلعة الحلة بالبريمي، ١٩٦٧

Bureimi, entrance to the Al Hilla fort, 1967.

قلعة الخندق بالبريمي، ١٩٦٢

Bureimi, Al Khandaq fort, 1962.

تقع واحة البريمي على حدود عمان مع دولة الإمارات العربية المتحدة وتحتل موقعا استراتيجيا يسهل من الوصول إلى ساحل الباطنة عبر وادي الجزي وإلى عبري ونزوى وإلى دولة الإمارات.

وتحولت البريمي خلال السنوات الثلاثين الماضية إلى مدينة حديثة مزودة بكل المرافق العصرية على أن هناك بعض القرى التقليدية التي لا تزال موجودة وسط مزارع النخيل .

مدخل قلعة الحلة البريمي، ٢٠٠٠

Bureimi, entrance to the Al Hilla fort, 2000.

مدخل قلعة الخندق بالبريمي، ٢٠٠٠

Bureimi, entrance to the Al Khandaq fort, 2000.

MAHDAH, the most northerly town of significance in the Dhahirah, is located some 30 kilometres northeast of Bureimi. It is the capital of the Beni Kaab and occupies a central position between the Batinah coast, Bureimi and the UAE.

منظر لمحضة، ١٩٦٧

Mahdah, outlook 1967.

قلعة بيت ناد بمحضة، مقر إقامة الشيخ عبدالله بن سالم الكعبي، ١٩٦٧

Mahdah, Bait Nad fort, residence of Sheikh Abdullah bin Salim Al Kaabi, 1967.

الحدود مع الإمارات العربية المتحدة في وادي الجزي، ١٩٧٢

Border with the UAE in the wadi *Jizzi, 1972.*

تقع مدينة محضة في أقصى منطقة الظاهرة على بعد نحو ٣٠ كيلومترا شمال شرق مدينة البريمي.
ومحضة هي مركز قبيلة بني كعب وتحتل موقعاً مركزيا بين ساحل الباطنة والبريمي ودولة الإمارات .

Mahdah, outlook, 2000. منظر لمحضة، ٢٠٠٠

أطلال قلعة بيت ناد بمحضة، ٢٠٠٠

Mahdah, remains of Bait Nad fort, 2000.

المسكن الجديد لشيخ بني كعب بمحضة، ٢٠٠٠

Mahdah, new residence of the Sheikh of the Beni Kaab, 2000.

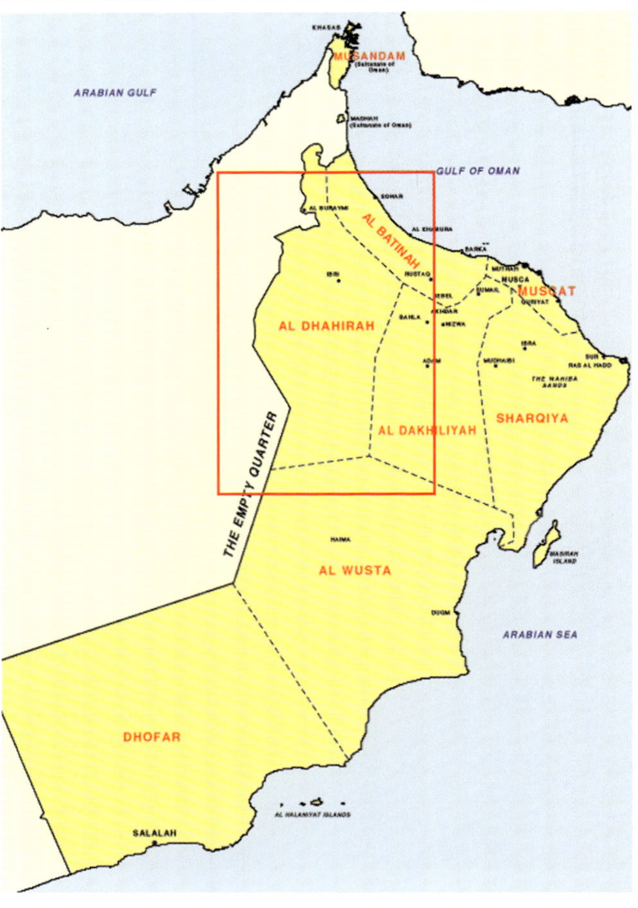

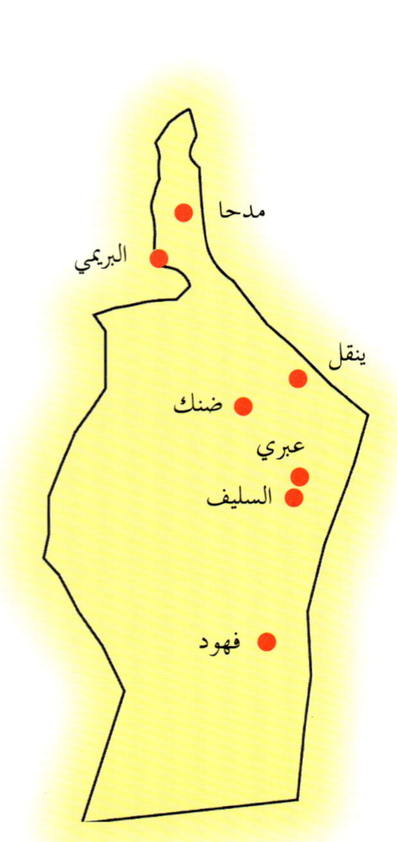

منطقة الظاهرة

تمثل منطقة الظاهرة الجزء الشمالي الغربي من السلطنة وتقع بين جبال الحجر الغربي وصحراء الربع الخالي وتمتد من محضة في الشمال وفهود في الجنوب مرورا بالبريمي وعبري وهي عبارة عن سهل شبه صحراوي. وعبري هي المدينة الرئيسية في منطقة الظاهرة وتقع غربي بهلا بنحو ١٠٠ كيلومترا . وتتصل منطقة الظاهرة بساحل الباطنة من خلال طريقين : عبر وادي الجزي من البريمي إلى صحار وعبر وادي الحواسنة من عبري إلى الخابورة. ومنطقة الظاهرة هي منطقة تمركز قبيلة الدروع وهي إحدى القبائل البدوية الرئيسية الأربع في عمان وتعد مدينة تنعم بالقرب من عبري من أهم مراكزهم . ويستوطن الدروع منطقة واسعة ويعتمدون في معيشتهم على تربية الإبل والأغنام والضأن ويتمركزون حول وادي العين ووادي الأسود ووادي العميري .

وبحكم أن الاكتشافات النفطية الرئيسية الأولى تمت في حقول فهود وجبال ونتيه التي تقع في حدود أراضيهم استفاد الدروع أكثر من سواهم من النفط وبخاصة من حيث توفر فرص العمل . وتعمل الحكومة على إعادة توطين الدروع وغيرهم من القبائل البدوية الأخرى في مناطق سكنية جديدة غير أن البعض منهم ما زالوا يفضلون حياتهم البدوية على الاستقرار .

Beehive burial tombs (c. 2500 BC) near Ibri

قبور على شكل خلية النحل (٢٥٠٠ قبل الميلاد) قرب عبري

Muskat Harbour from the Fisher-men's Rock (R. Temple 1809-1810).

ميناء مسقط من صخرة الصيادين (آر تمبل ١٨٠٩-١٨١٠)

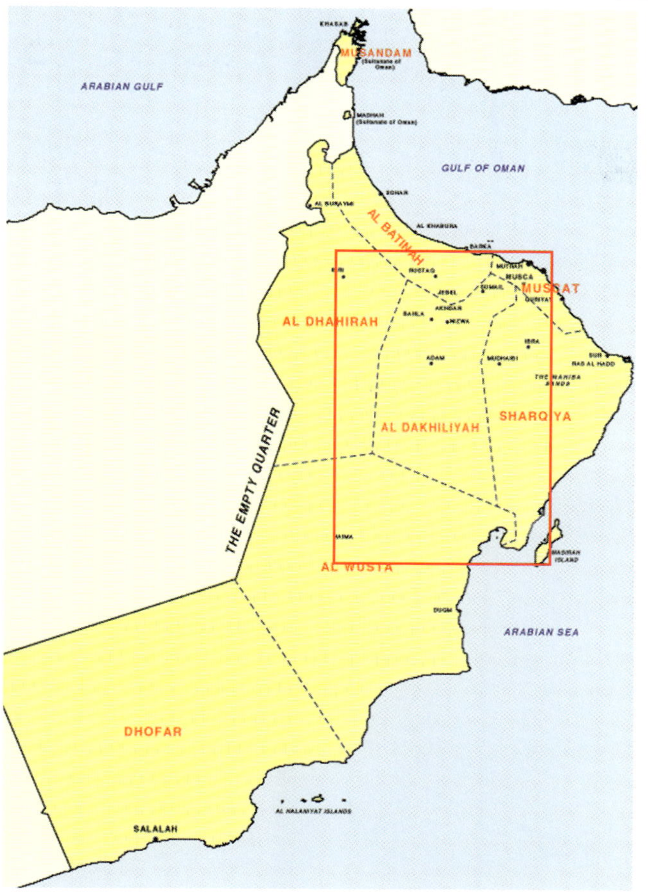

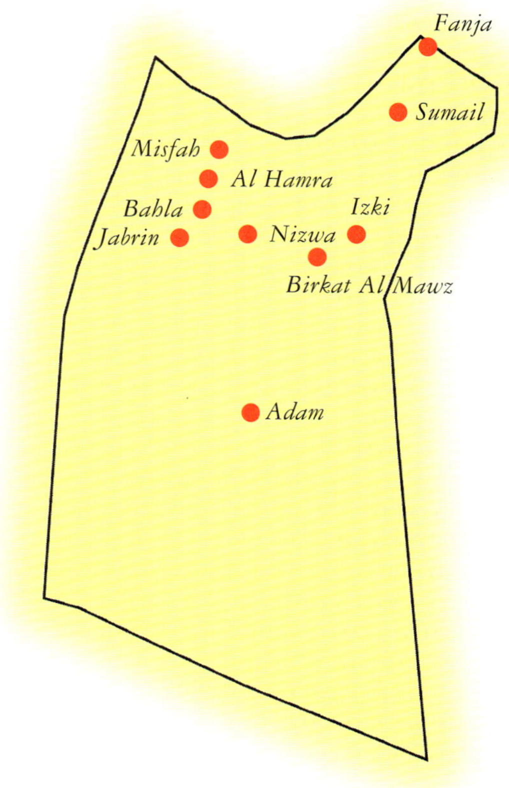

Al Dakhiliyah

The Al Dakhiliyah province lies to the west of the Hajar Mountains. Previously called the "Al Jauf", this area forms the geographical core of Oman. It stretches from Bahla in the northwest via the Jebel Akhdar Mountains to Izki, and further south to well beyond Adam. Also part of this province is the Sumail gap from Izki to Fanja, the principal travel route from the interior to coastal Oman.

Al Dakhiliyah has played a dominant role throughout the history of Oman. The principal town of Dakhiliyah, both in the past and today, is Nizwa, which at various times in its history has been the capital of the Imamate of Oman.

Sumail gap, wadi *Sumail near Bid Bid, 1972.*

وادي سمائل قرب بدبد، ١٩٧٢

قرية منال بفجوة سمائل تحرسها سبعة أبراج مراقبة، ٢٠٠٠

Sumail gap, Manal village guarded by seven watchtowers, 2000.

Sumail gap, Al Muhal village, old and new combined, 2000.

قرية المحل بفجوة سمائل تجمع القديم والحديث، ٢٠٠٠

قرية بركة الموز على سفح الجبل، ١٩٩٩

Birkat Al Mawz village nestling against the mountain, 1999.

Entrance to the wadi *Muaydin behind Birkat Al Mawz, 1972.*

مدخل وادي المعيدن خلف بركة الموز، ١٩٧٢

FANJA, is a fortified village at the seaside entrance of the Sumail gap. This gap provides the principal route through the Hajar mountains between the coast and the interior.

منظر عام لفنجاء، ١٩٧٣

View of Fanja, 1973.

سيارة تابعة للشركة تعبر وادي فنجاء، ١٩٧٣

Fanja, a PDO vehicle crossing the wadi, *1973.*

تعد فنجاء قرية محصنة تقع على مدخل فجوة سمائل من جهة البحر. وتوفر الفجوة الطريق الرئيسي الذي يربط الساحل بالمنطقة الداخلية مرورا بجبال الحجر.

مدينة فنجاء من الطريق الرئيسي، ١٩٩٩

Fanja, townscape from the main road, 1999.

Fanja, a large viaduct passes over the wadi, *2000.*

جسر فنجاء عبر الوادي، ٢٠٠٠

SUMAIL, which lends its name to the pass, is a collective name for some twelve villages set in extensive palm groves and market gardens along the *wadi* Sumail, one of the larger *wadi*s in Oman. Perched on a hilltop in Upper Sumail stands an imposing fort complex, built by the same architect who designed the castle in Rustaq.

The Sumail area is famous for the quality of its dates, which used to be exported in quantity to the USA until the Americans began their own date cultivation in California.

قلعة سمائل، ١٩٦٨

Sumail fort, 1968.

قرية سمائل العلوية تحت القلعة، ١٩٦٨

Upper Sumail village below the fort, 1968.

Wadi *Sumail, 1972. In the background, the Jebel Akhdar mountains.*

وادي سمائل، ١٩٧٢، ويظهر في الخلف الجبل الأخضر

تضم سمائل نحو اثنتي عشرة قرية وتقع وسط مزارع واسعة من النخيل والحدائق الممتدة عبر وادي سمائل الذي يعد أحد أكبر الأودية في عمان. وتوجد قلعة كبيرة فوق تل جبلي في سمائل العليا شيدها نفس المهندس الذي صمم حصن الرستاق. وتشتهر سمائل بجودة تمورها والتي كانت تصدر إلى الولايات المتحدة بكميات كبيرة إلى أن بدأ الأمريكان زراعة أشجار النخيل في ولاية كاليفورنيا.

قلعة سمائل، ٢٠٠٠

Sumail fort, 2000.

قرية سمائل، ٢٠٠٠

Sumail village, 2000.

Wadi *Sumail, 2000.*

وادي سمائل، ٢٠٠٠

قرية الجيلة في فجوة سمائل، ١٩٧٢

Al Jaylah village in the Sumail gap, 1972.

Izki, 1969. Located at the entrance to the Sumail gap on the interior side, Izki comprises a group of villages perched on the edge of the wadi *Halfayn.*

إزكي ١٩٦٩، تقع على مدخل فجوة سمائل صوب المنطقة الداخلية وتتكون من مجموعة من القرى تقع على حافة وادي حلفين

الطريق الرئيسي عبر فجوة سمائل، ١٩٦٩

Main road through the Sumail gap, 1969.

قرية الجيلة في فجوة
سمائل، ٢٠٠٠

Al Jaylah village in the Sumail gap, 2000.

مشروع ازدواجية الطريق الرئيسي
عبر فجوة سمائل، ٢٠٠٠

Highway through the Sumail gap being expanded from two to four lanes, 2000.

إزكي القديمة ووادي حلفين، ٢٠٠٠

Old Izki and the wadi *Halfayn, 2000.*

يتوسط مدينة إزكي الجديدة طريق سمائل الرئيسي، ٢٠٠٠

The new town of Izki centred around the Sumail highway, 2000.

بركة الموز تقع على مدخل وادي المعيدين، ١٩٧٢. وإلى اليسار أطلال القلعة التي تعرضت للقصف أثناء حرب الجبل (١٩٥٤-١٩٥٩).

Birkat Al Mawz lying at the entrance to the wadi *Muaydin, 1972. To the left are the ruins of the fort bombed during the Jebel War (1954-1959).*

برج المراقبة في بركة الموز وأدناه فلجها المشهور، ١٩٦٦

Birkat Al Mawz watchtower with below, the famous falaj*, 1966.*

ثلاث نساء من بركة الموز يحملن جرار الماء قرب الفلج

Birkat Al Mawz, three women carrying water jars near the falaj.

Birkat Al Mawz, outlook, 1999. On the left, the entrance to the wadi *Muaydin and the renovated fort; on the right, the watchtower.*

منظر عام لبركة الموز، ١٩٩٩. إلى اليسار مدخل وادي المعيدن والقلعة التي تم ترميمها وإلى اليمين برج المراقبة.

Birkat Al Mawz, children near the falaj*, 1996.*

أطفال من بركة الموز قرب الفلج، ١٩٩٦

NIZWA is the administrative and residential centre of Dakhiliyah. The town, well protected by the Jebel Akhdar Mountains and fed by the waters of the two most prolific *falaj*es in Oman (F. Daris and F. Ghandaq), was a natural choice for capital of the Imamate. Divided into two sections by the *wadi* Kalbu, Nizwa is set in vast date groves, grouped around an enormous circular fort tower. Some 65,000 inhabitants, a six-fold increase compared to 1970, live in Nizwa and its surrounding areas and are, for the most part, farmers and traders. The suq at Nizwa, once made up of many shaded, narrow, interconnecting streets with hundreds of small shops, has been renovated and is now housed in a modern arcade. Nizwa has always been noted for its silver jewellery and copper ware, in particular, the famous Nizwa coffee pots.

Nizwa fort viewed from the south, 1966. The fort is dominated by a 34-m high, circular tower, built by Sultan bin Said al Ya-rubi between 1670 and 1680.

منظر لقلعة نزوى من الجنوب، ١٩٦٦. ويبلغ طول برج القلعة ٣٤ متراً وقام ببنائها الإمام سلطان بن سيف اليعربي بين عامي ١٦٧٠ و١٦٨٠.

نزوى هي المركز الإداري والسكني للمنطقة الداخلية. وتحمى المدينة سلسلة جبال الجبل الأخضر وتأخذ نزوى حاجتها من المياه من أغزر فلجين وهما فلج دارس وفلج الغنتق. وكانت نزوى هي العاصمة المختارة للإمامة. ويقسم وادي كلبوه المدينة إلى جزءين وتتوسط المدينة مزارع واسعة من أشجار النخيل وقلعة ضخمة دائرية الشكل وبها برج للمراقبة. ويبلغ تعداد سكان المدينة وما حولها من مناطق نحو ٦٥٠٠٠ نسمة أي ستة أضعاف ما كان عليه الوضع عام ١٩٧٠. ويعمل معظم السكان في الزراعة والتجارة. وقد تم تحديث سوق المدينة الذي يشتهر فيما يشتهر بالمصوغات الفضية والمصنوعات النحاسية المختلفة بما فيها ركوة القهوة الشهيرة.

منظر لقلعة نزوى ومسجدها وسوقها الجديد، ١٩٩٩

Nizwa, overview of fort, mosque and new suq, as seen from the south, 1999.

حارس أمام مدخل قلعة نزوى، ١٩٧٦

Nizwa, Askari guarding the entrance to the fort, 1976.

جمال تنزل حمولتها من الفحم قرب قلعة نزوى، ١٩٦٨

Nizwa, camels offloading charcoal near the fort, 1968.

داخل برج قلعة نزوى الدائري، ١٩٧٢

Nizwa, inside the circular tower fort, 1972.

اللقطة رقم ٢٠: منظر عام لمحطة الغاز في جبال ١٩٩٩

Nizwa, Friday second-hand car market, 1999.

داخل برج القلعة، ١٩٩٩

Nizwa, inside the tower fort, 1999.

منظر من برج قلعة نزوى نحو الجبل الأخضر، ١٩٧٢

Nizwa, view from the tower towards the Jebel Akhdar Mountains, 1972.

منظر من برج قلعة نزوى عبر المدينة والواحة، ١٩٧٢

Nizwa, view from the tower over the town and the oasis, 1972.

منظر من برج القلعة نحو الجبل الأخضر، ١٩٩٩

Nizwa, view from the tower towards the Jebel Akhdar Mountains, 1999.

منظر من برج القلعة لجامع السلطان
قابوس بنزوى والمدينة، ١٩٩٩

Nizwa, view from the tower of the new Sultan Qaboos Mosque and town, 1999.

مدخل سوق نزوى، ١٩٧٦

Nizwa, entrance to the suq, 1976.

سوق نزوى، ١٩٧٠

Nizwa, market, 1970.

Nizwa, view of the town and the fort from the north, 1972.

منظر للمدينة ولقلعة نزوى من الشمال، ١٩٧٢

أجزاء من سوق نزوى القديم، ١٩٩٩

Remaining part of the old Nizwa suq, 1999.

ركوات القهوة التقليدية في سوق نزوى الجديد، ١٩٩٩

New Nizwa suq, antique coffee pots, 1999.

قسط من الراحة بعد التسوق في سوق نزوى الشرقي، ١٩٩٩

Nizwa East suq, taking a rest after shopping, 1999.

Nizwa, the town, the fort and the mosque, viewed from the north, 1999.

منظر لمدينة نزوى والقلعة والمسجد من الشمال، ١٩٩٩

فتاة تتزين بمصوغات فضية تقليدية
من الأقراط والعقد المطرز بالقروش
الفضية، ١٩٩٧

Girl wearing traditional silver jewellery, including earrings (halaq) *and a necklace with Maria Theresa thalers, 1997.*

فتاة تتزين بحرف منقوش من الفضة، ١٩٦٨

Girl with traditional silver head decoration, 1968.

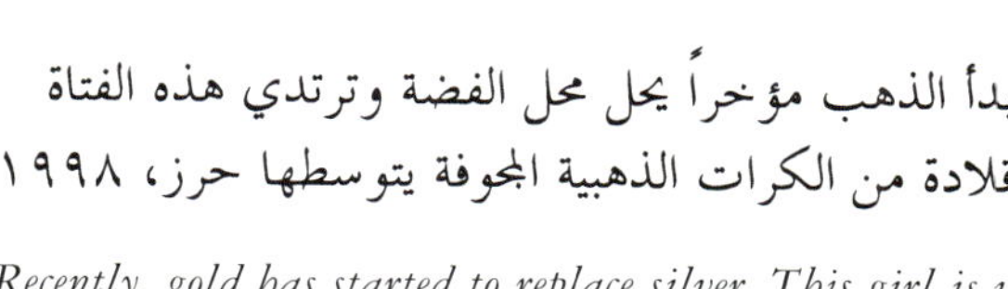

بدأ الذهب مؤخراً يحل محل الفضة وترتدي هذه الفتاة
قلادة من الكرات الذهبية المجوفة يتوسطها حرز، ١٩٩٨

Recently, gold has started to replace silver. This girl is wearing a necklace of hollow gold beads and a Quran Box (hirz), *1998.*

فتاة من المسفاة، ١٩٩٩

Girl from Misfah, 1999.

AL HAMRA, located to the north of Bahla on the lower slopes of the Jebel Akhdar Mountains, is one of the most elegant towns in Oman with its multi-storied houses and terraced gardens.

الشارع الرئيسي في الحمراء، ١٩٦٨

Al Hamra, main street, 1968.

منظر عام للحمراء، ١٩٧٦

View of Al Hamra, 1976.

فتاة من الحمراء تحمل دلو ماء، ١٩٧٦

Al Hamra, girl carrying water, 1976.

بيوت متعددة الطوابق في الحمراء، ١٩٧٦

Multi-storey houses in Al Hamra, 1976.

تقع مدينة الحمراء شمال بهلا على منحدر الجبل الأخضر وهي من بين أكثر المدن العمانية روعة وتتميز ببيوتها المتعددة الطوابق ومزارعها الخضراء.

الحمراء حديثاً وقديماً حيث يظهر جبل وال في الخلف، ١٩٩٩

Old and new Al Hamra with the Jebel Waal in the background, 1999.

الشارع الرئيسي في الحمراء، ١٩٩٩

Al Hamra, main street, 1999.

امرأة تمر من أمام بيت تقليدي في الحمراء، ١٩٩٩

Woman in front of traditional house in Al Hamra, 1999.

باب منحوت في الحمراء، ١٩٩٩

Al Hamra, carved door, 1999.

MISFAH is situated uphill from Al Hamra. It is a typical *jebel* village, with the houses clinging to the steep hillsides and being built of stone instead of mud.

منظر عام للمسفاة، ١٩٧٦

Misfah, panorama, 1976.

زقاق في المسفاة به درج، ١٩٧٦

Misfah, alleyway with staircase, 1976.

فتيات من المسفاة أمام بيوت عالية، ١٩٧٦

Misfah, girls in front of fortified houses, 1976.

Misfah, entrance route to the village, 1976.

طريق المدخل إلى قرية المسفاة، ١٩٧٦

تقع قرية المسفاه في أعلى الجبل من الحمراء. وهي قرية جبلية نموذجية، حيث تستقر بيوتها، المبنية بالحصى بدلا من الطوب، على جوانب الجبل شديدة الانحدار.

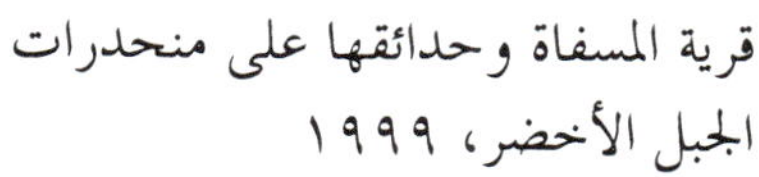

قرية المسفاة وحدائقها على منحدرات الجبل الأخضر، ١٩٩٩

Misfah, village and gardens nestling against the slopes of the Jebel Akhdar Mountains, 1999.

الطريق الجديد إلى المسفاة، ١٩٩٩

Misfah, new access road, 1999.

فتيات من المسفاة أمام بيوت محصنة، ١٩٩٩

Misfah, girls in front of fortified houses, 1999.

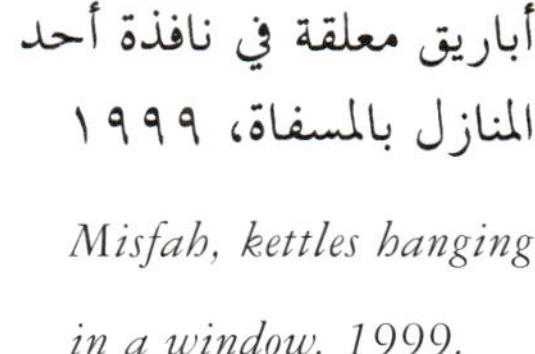

أباريق معلقة في نافذة أحد المنازل بالمسفاة، ١٩٩٩

Misfah, kettles hanging in a window, 1999.

The town of Bahla lies 40 kilometres to the west of Nizwa, and once was the capital of Oman. Dominating the town is a massive fort built by the Nabahina rulers and now listed by UNESCO as a World Heritage Site.

منظر عام لبهلا من الجنوب، ١٩٦٦ وفي الوسط تبدو قلعة بهلا المهيبة (حصن الطماح)، كما يبدو في صدر الصورة جزء من السور المبني بالطوب ويبلغ طوله ١٢ كم وكان يوماً ما يحيط بالمدينة.

Bahla, view from the south, 1966. In the centre, the imposing fort (Hisn Tahwah); in the foreground, part of the 12-km wall of mud bricks that once surrounded the town.

Bahla fort, 1973. قلعة بهلا، ١٩٧٣

تقع مدينة بهلا غربي نزوى بنحو ٤٠ كم وكانت عاصمة لعمان. وتتميز بقلعتها الشامخة التي بناها النباهنة وفي الوقت الحاضر أدرجتها منظمة اليونسكو ضمن مواقع التراث العالمي التي يجب صونها.

منظر لبهلا من الجنوب، ١٩٩٩

Bahla, view taken from the south, 1999.

قلعة بهلا وسورها، ١٩٩٦

Bahla, wall and fort, 1996.

Bahla, townscape from the north, 1999.

منظر لبهلا من الشمال، ١٩٩٩

شجرة ضخمة تتوسط سوق بهلا، ١٩٧٦
The Bahla suq centered around a massive tree, 1976.

صناعة الفخار في بهلا، ١٩٧٣. وإلى اليمين
يبدو الفرن الذي تحرق فيه الأواني الفخارية
Bahla, pottery industry, 1973. On the right, the oven.

Typical Bahla pots, 1976.
أواني فخارية نموذجية
من بهلا، ١٩٧٦

Bahla, preparing pots for transport, 1973.
إعداد الأواني للنقل، ١٩٧٣

سوق بهلا القديم، ١٩٩٩. انقسمت الشجرة المشهورة إلى جزأين ولكنها مازالت باقية.

The old Bahla suq, 1999. The famous tree has split in two, but is still alive.

أحد الأفران التي مازالت صامدة ١٩٩٨

Bahla, one of the surviving pottery ovens, 1998.

التصاميم الحديثة لفخاريات بهلا، ١٩٩٨

Bahla pots, modern designs, 1998.

The town of Adam lies some 70 kilometres south of Bahla, well into the gravel plains of the desert. Finding a town the size of Adam so far from the Hajar Mountains is due to the fact that it is surrounded by three sizeable *jebel*s of its own (Salakh, Khamila, Mudh'maar), from which the town's *falaj*es draw water. Another of Adam's distinctions is that the founder of the Al Bu Said dynasty came from there.

مدخل أدم، ١٩٧١

Entering Adam, 1971.

أدم، ١٩٧١، حيث يبدو جبل مضمار في الخلف

Adam, 1971, with Jebel Mudh'maar in the background.

حدائق داخل الواحة، ١٩٧١

Adam, gardens inside the oasis, 1971.

تقع مدينة أدم جنوبي بهلا بنحو ٧٠ كيلو مترا وتمتد إلى السهول الحصبائية في الصحراء. وتوجد في المدينة التي تقع بعيدا عن جبال الحجر ثلاثة جبال كبيرة هي صمخ وخميلة ومضمار وهي تمد الأفلاج بكفايتها من المياه. ويذكر أن مؤسس أسرة البوسعيد جاء من هذه المدينة.

منظر من الغرب لشمال أدم وجنوبها، ١٩٩٩

Adam, view from the west, 1999.

مزارع أدم وجبل مضمار، ٢٠٠٠

Adam gardens and Jebel Mudh'maar, 2000.

Adam, view taken from the east, 2000. Jebel Khamila in the background.

منظر لأدم من الشرق، ٢٠٠٠
ويبدو جبل خميلة في الخلف

بوابة أدم، ١٩٦٢ *Adam, town gate, 1962.*

زقاق داخل واحة أدم، ١٩٦٢

Adam, alley inside the oasis, 1962.

بئر ماء في أدم، ١٩٦٤

Adam, water well, 1964.

بوابة أدم، ٢٠٠٠

Adam, town gate, 2000.

زقاق داخل واحة أدم، ٢٠٠٠

Adam, alley inside the oasis, 2000.

بئر ماء في أدم، ٢٠٠٠
حلت المضخات محل العمال

Adam, water well, 2000. Pumps have replaced manual labour.

Adam, Saif bin Mohammed (second from left) and Salim bin Hamed Al Mahrouqi (third from left) in front of gate, 1971.

أدم، سيف بن محمد (الثاني إلى اليسار) وسالم بن حمد المحروقي (الثالث إلى اليسار) أمام البوابة ، ١٩٧١

Adam, Saif bin Mohammed (seated at left) and Salim bin Hamed Al Mahrouqi (second from left) with son and grandson in front of the gate, 2000.

أدم، سيف بن محمد (الجالس إلى اليسار) وسالم بن حمد المحروقي (الثاني إلى اليسار) مع أحد الأبناء والأحفاد أمام البوابة ، ٢٠٠٠

شروق الشمس على جبل شمس، أعلى
جبل في عمان (٢٩٨٠ مترا)، ١٩٩٨

Sunset over the Jebel Shams, the highest mountain (2980 m) in Oman, 1998.

قلعة جبرين، ١٩٩٦ بناها الإمام بلعرب بن سلطان
اليعربي عام ١٦٨٨. وتم تصميمها بشكل جميل بحيث
تفي بمهمتها الدفاعية ولتكون مركزاً لتدريس القانون
والطب وعلم التنجيم.

Jabrin Castle near Bahla, 1996. Built in 1688 by Imam Bilarub bin Sultan Al Ya-rubi, it is a beautifully designed building, combining a defensive function with one of learning, notably of law, medicine, and astrology.

منح، ١٩٩٩. تقع في منتصف الطريق بين نزوى وأدم. وكانت منح محطة مهمة في طرق القوافل التي تستخدم الجمال في رحلاتها من الشمال إلى الجنوب. وأصبحت المدينة القديمة مهجورة الآن وشيدت حولها مدينة حديثة.

Manah, 1999. Located half-way between Nizwa and Adam, Manah was once an important station on the north-south camel caravan routes. The old town is now deserted and a modern replacement has sprung up around it.

مسجد قديم في أدم، ٢٠٠٠

Adam, ancient mosque, 2000.

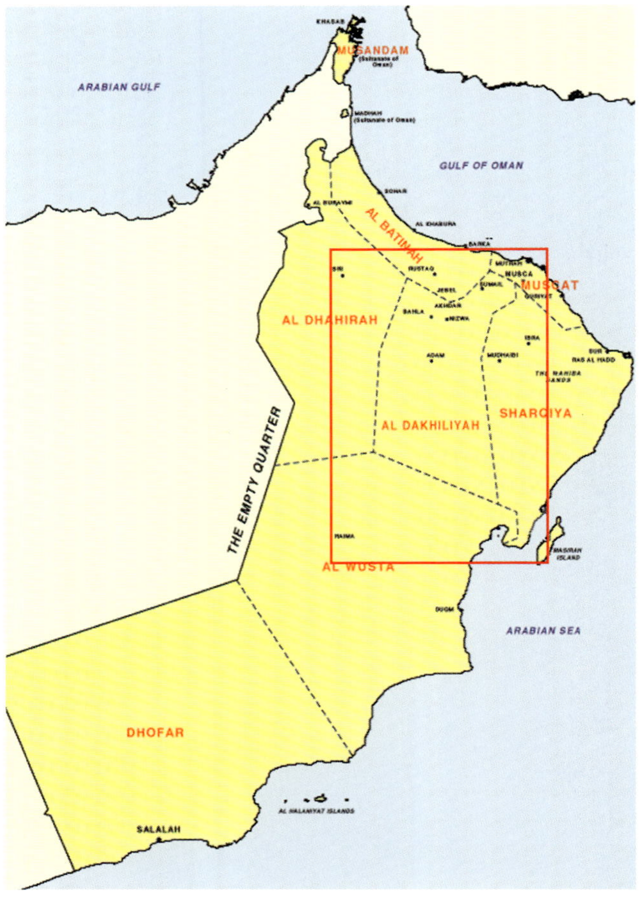

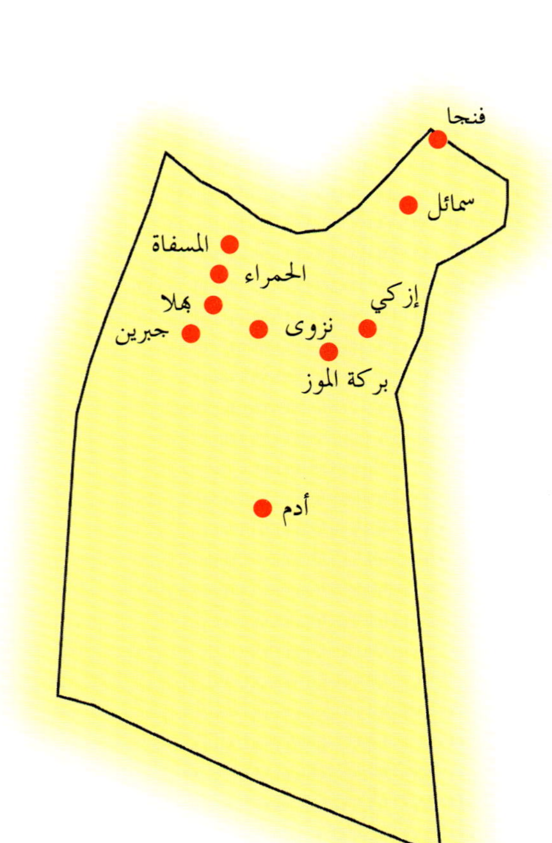

المنطقة الداخلية

تقع المنطقة الداخلية إلى الغرب من جبال الحجر. وكانت المنطقة تعرف فيما مضى بمنطقة "الجوف" وهي تمثل المركز الجغرافي لعمان. وتمتد من بهلا في الشمال الغربي عبر قمم الجبل الأخضر إلى إزكي فجنوبا إلى ما وراء أدم. وتقع في هذه المنطقة فجوة سمائل وتمتد من إزكي إلى فنجاء ويمر بها الطريق الرئيسي من الداخلية إلى ساحل عمان.

ولعبت المنطقة الداخلية دورا بارزا في تاريخ عمان وظلت نزوى هي المدينة الرئيسية في المنطقة الداخلية في الماضي والحاضر وكانت عاصمة للإمامة في أوقات مختلفة من تاريخها.

Muskat from the Harbour (R. Temple 1809-1810). مسقط من الميناء (آر تمبل ١٨٠٩ – ١٨١٠)

Schinaafs from the Sea (R. Temple 1809-1810)

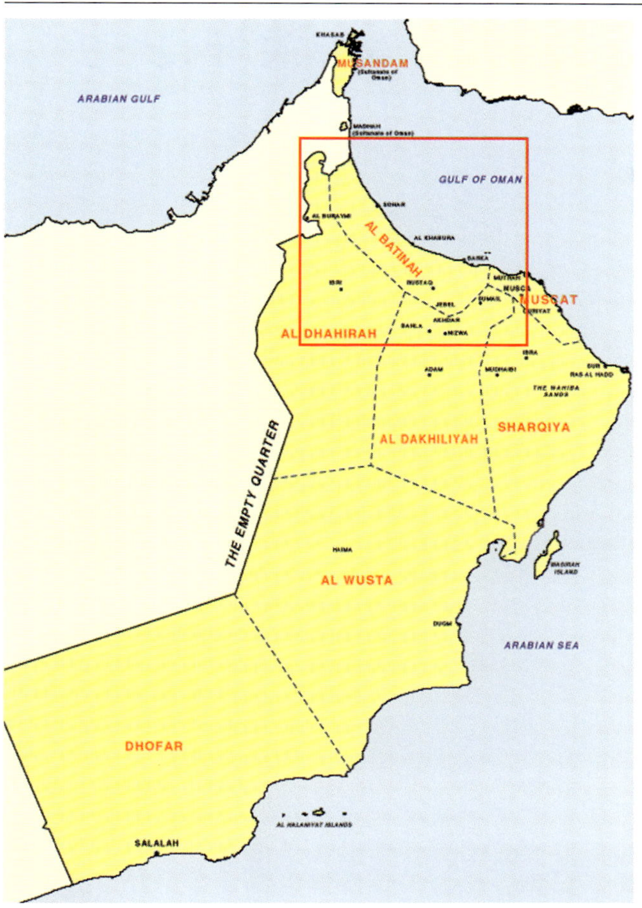

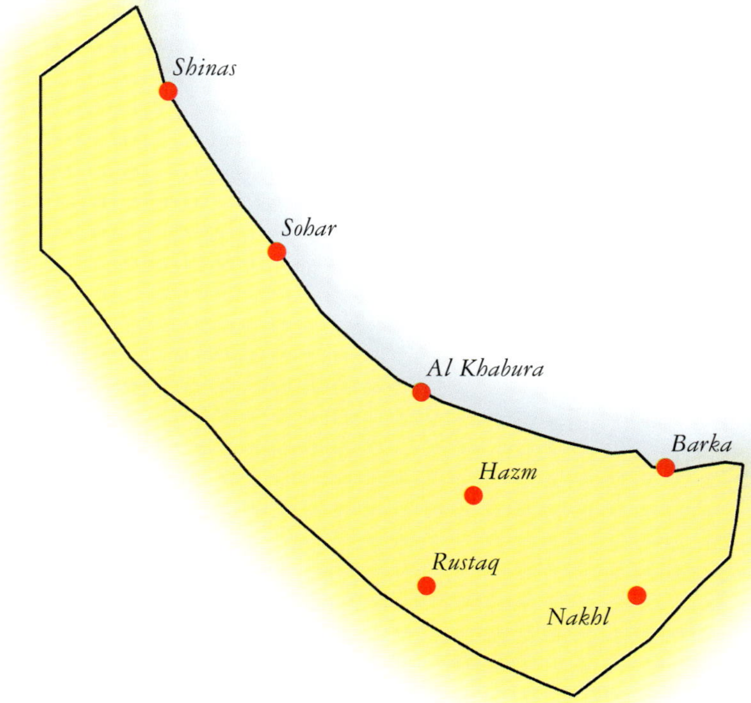

Al Batinah

The Batinah province comprises the crescent-shaped coastal area extending from the Oman border with the UAE in the north to halfway between the towns of Barka and Seeb in the south. To the east, it is bounded by the Gulf of Oman and, to the west, it is bordered by the seaward side of the Western Hajar Mountains. The Batinah area and, in particular, the principal towns of Sohar, Barka and Rustaq, has played a significant role in the history of Oman.

One of the main assets of the Batinah area is fresh water, which is derived from the relatively shallow natural subterranean flows from the Hajar Mountains. As a consequence, the Batinah area is largely fertile and provides Oman and other countries in the region with a significant percentage of their fresh fruit (in particular, limes and dates), vegetables and, more recently, dairy produce. The other important asset of the Batinah is its easy access to a sea teeming with a wide variety of excellent edible fish. With very few harbours along the coast, fishing has generally remained a small-scale operation, although outboard-powered polyester boats have replaced the traditional *huris*.

About one quarter of the total population of the country lives in the Batinah, with Sohar as its capital.

Batinah beach, 1964. Until 1970, the beach was one of the best routes to travel, in particular at low tide.

ساحل الباطنة ١٩٦٤. حتى عام ١٩٧٠ كان الساحل من أفضل الطرق للسفر وخاصة عند الجزر.

وادي الحواسنة ١٩٦٩. يعتبر هذا الوادي واحداً من الطرق القليلة التي توصل ساحل الباطنة بالمنطقة الداخلية. ويلتقي بالبحر في ولاية الخابورة.

The wadi *Hawasina, 1969. This* wadi *is one of the few passes connecting the Batinah coast with the Interior. It opens up to the sea at Al Khaboura.*

وادي الحواسنة، ١٩٧٣ السلسلة التي شدّها ليز عام ١٩٢٨ (راجع فصل تاريخ صناعة النفط والغاز في عمان)

Wadi *Hawasina, Chain of Lees, 1973. This chain was installed in 1928 (see chapter on the history of oil and gas in Oman).*

قرية تقليدية قرب الرستاق مع بيوت مبنية من الطين وقلعة ومزارع وبئر ماء، ١٩٧٨

Traditional village near Rustaq with mud houses, fort, gardens and water well, 1978.

قرية حديثة في وادي بني غافر، ١٩٩٩

Modern village in the wadi *Bani Ghafir, 1999.*

SOHAR, located just south of the Straits of Hormuz and at the mouth of the *wadi* Jizzi, is the oldest town of any significance in Oman. Already in the third millennium BC, Sohar was a transit port for goods, notably copper and building materials, brought in from the Interior for onward transport to Dilmun (Bahrain) and Mesopotamia. Also, at the time of the Persian reign (Sassanid period) and early Islam, Sohar was a large port with over 12,000 houses and a cosmopolitan population. It reached its zenith during the tenth century, when trade with India and Africa thrived. In the 14th century, Sohar became part of the kingdom of Hormuz and, in the 15th century, was captured by the Portuguese, after which its fortunes started to decline. After the Portuguese were ousted from Oman, Sohar continued to play a role, but as trade with India and Africa had meanwhile moved to Muscat and Sur, it never regained its former splendour and influence.

With the exception of the beautifully restored fort, little remains of the past and, today, Sohar is a pleasant, modern town.

منظر لصحار من الجنوب، ١٩٧٢. وفي الوسط يبدو مكتب الوالي

Sohar, view from the south, 1972. In the centre, the wali*'s office.*

قلعة صحار، ١٩٧٢. يعود تاريخ بناء هذه القلعة إلى القرن العاشر الميلادي. وقام البرتغاليون بإدخال تعديلات واسعة عليها في القرن السادس عشر الميلادي، وكذلك العمانيون بعد ذلك.

Sohar fort, 1972. The origins of this fort date back to the tenth century. It was extensively modified by the Portuguese in the 16th century, and later by the Omanis.

تقع صحار التي تعد أقدم مدينة عمانية مشهورة جنوبي مضيق هرمز وفي مدخل وادي الجزي. ففي الألفية الثالثة قبل الميلاد كانت صحار معروفة كميناء لتصدير مختلف البضائع وأشهرها النحاس ومواد البناء التي كانت تجلب من المنطقة الداخلية لتصديرها إلى ديلمون (البحرين) وبلاد ما بين النهرين. وفي عصر الفرس (فترة الساسانيين) وفي فجر الإسلام كانت صحار ميناء كبيرا يضم أكثر من ١٢ ألف مسكن وسكانا من مختلف الجنسيات. وبلغت صحار أوج عظمتها خلال القرن العاشر عندما ازدهرت التجارة مع الهند وأفريقيا. وفي خلال القرن الرابع عشر أصبحت صحار جزءا من مملكة هرمز وفي القرن الخامس عشر احتلها البرتغاليون وبعد ذلك بدأت ثروات صحار تضمحل. وبعد طرد البرتغاليين من عمان ظلت صحار تلعب دورا هاما ولكن ومع انتقال النشاط التجاري مع الهند وأفريقيا إلى مسقط وصور في تلك الأثناء، لم تستعد صحار أبدا مكانتها ونفوذها السابق.

وتضم الآثار القديمة في صحار القلعة التي تم ترميمها ترميما جميلا وبعض الآثار الأخرى. وتعد صحار اليوم مدينة عصرية جميلة.

منظر لصحار من المسجد، ١٩٩٩
وفي الوسط تبدو القلعة شامخة.

Sohar, view from the mosque, 1999. In the centre, the splendid fort.

مكتب والي صحار، ١٩٩٩

Sohar, wali's office, 1999.

قلعة صحار التي تم ترميمها بشكل جميل، ١٩٩٩

Sohar fort, beautifully restored, 1999.

Camel caravan near Sohar, 1967.

قافلة جمال قرب صحار، ١٩٦٧

AL KHABURA is one of the many fishing villages typical of the Batinah coast. Surrounded by extensive palm groves, orchards and gardens, it is built at the mouth of the *wadi* Hawasina. Camel races are regularly held in the area.

قرية الخابورة وبيوتها النموذجية المبنية بسعف النخيل، ١٩٧٢

Al Khabura village with typical barasti *houses, 1972.*

قافلة جمال قرب صحار، ١٩٩٩

Camel caravan near Sohar, 1999.

تعتبر الخابورة إحدى المدن التي تشتهر بمهنة الصيد شأنها شأن المدن الأخرى على ساحل الباطنة. وبنيت المدينة التي تحيط بها بساتين النخيل ومزارع أشجار الفاكهة على مصب وادي الحواسنة. وتقام في المنطقة سباقات الهجن بانتظام.

قرية الخابورة، ١٩٩٩

Al Khabura village, 1999.

AS SUWAIQ, located about halfway between Al Khabura and Barka, is one of the few fishing villages along the Batinah coast with an active port. It also has an imposing fort.

As Suwaiq fort and market, 1967.

قلعة السويق وسوقها، ١٩٦٧

Tharmad fort, located some 10 km east of As Suwaiq, 1972.

قلعة ثرمد التي تبعد حوالي ١٠ كم غربي السويق، ١٩٧٢

تقع السويق في منتصف المسافة بين الخابورة وبركاء وتعد واحدة من قرى الصيد القليلة الموجودة على طول ساحل الباطنة وبها ميناء ذو حركة نشطة. وتوجد بها أيضا قلعة كبيرة.

As Suwaiq fort and market, 1999.

قلعة السويق وسوقها، ١٩٩٩

Tharmad fort, 1999.

قلعة ثرمد، ١٩٩٩

صيد السردين قرب
بركاء، ١٩٧٢

Sardine fishing near Barka, 1972.

قوارب الصيد المعروفة بالهوري وشيء
من الأسماك التي صيدت، المصنعة، ١٩٧٨

Huri *fishing boats and remains of the catch, Al Masna-ah, 1978.*

قوارب الشيشة التقليدية المصنوعة من
جريد النخيل والقوارب الحديثة في
شناص، ١٩٩٨

Traditional palm-frond 'shasha' *and modern polyester fishing boat at Shinas, 1998.*

حقول متدرجة على هضبة سيق، ١٩٩٨

Terraced fields near the Saiq Plateau, 1998.

حراثة الأرض في وادي بني غافر، ١٩٧٩

Wadi *Bani Ghafir, ploughing the fields, 1979.*

مربي النحل في وادي بني عوف يتفقد خلايا النحل المصنوعة من جذوع النخيل المجوفة، ١٩٧٨

A beekeeper in the wadi *Bani Awf tends his hollow palm-trunk hives, 1978.*

جني الرطب قرب الرستاق، ١٩٩٧

Harvesting dates near Rustaq, 1997.

Women and children at Rustaq, 1995. امرأتان وطفلان بالرستاق، ١٩٩٥

شيخ من الرستاق، ١٩٧٢
Old man at Rustaq, 1972.

الاستحمام في وادي السحتن، ١٩٩٩
Taking a bath, wadi *Sahtan, 1999.*

طفلتان من وادي بني غافر ١٩٨٠
Young girls, wadi *Bani Ghafir, 1980.*

سوق الماشية
قرب نخل، ٢٠٠٠

Goat market near Nakhl, 2000.

في انتظار زبون

Waiting for a buyer.

صفقة أبرمت

Sale concluded.

سباق الهجن قرب
الخابورة، ١٩٨١

Camel races near Al Khabura, 1981.

مصارعة الثيران قرب بركاء، ١٩٩٨

Bullfighting at Barka, 1998.

The Hazm oasis is located where the Batinah coastal plain meets the Hajar Mountains. Similar to many other places, Hazm is dominated by a large fort, built in 1708 by Imam Sultan bin Saif II of the Yaruba dynasty who, in 1711, moved the capital from Rustaq to Hazm. He was buried there in 1718. The Hazm fort is truly military, incorporating many state-of-the-art feats of engineering. Beautifully restored, it competes with the fort at Jabrin to be the most impressive in Oman.

Hazm fort, 1972. قلعة الحزم، ١٩٧٢

حارس في قلعة الحزم، ١٩٥٩

Guard at Hazm fort, 1959.

ممر داخلي في قلعة الحزم، ١٩٧٢

Hazm fort, inner passageway, 1972.

مدافع برتغالية استولى عليها العمانيون في القرن السابع عشر، ١٩٧٢

Hazm fort, Portuguese cannon captured by the Omanis in the 17th century, 1972.

تقع واحة الحزم في المكان الذي يلتقي فيه سهل الباطنة الساحلي جبال الحجر. وتوجد في الحزم قلعة كبيرة شيدها عام ١٧٠٨ الإمام سلطان بن سيف اليعربي الذي نقل عاصمته في ١٧١١ من الرستاق إلى الحزم كما هو الحال في العديد من الأماكن الأخرى. ودفن الإمام سلطان هناك عام ١٧١٨.

وتتميز قلعة الحزم بمزاياها العسكرية كما تضم جوانب هندسية رائعة. وبعد ترميمها أضحت قلعة الحزم تنافس قلعة جبرين في كونها القلعة الأفخم في عمان.

قلعة الحزم، ١٩٩٩

Hazm fort, 1999.

بوابة قلعة الحزم منقوشة بشكل جميل، ١٩٩٩

Beautifully carved and decorated entrance doors to Hazm fort, 1999.

ممر داخلي في قلعة الحزم، ١٩٩٩

Hazm fort, inner passage way, 1999.

مدافع البرتغاليين في قلعة الحزم، ١٩٩٨

Hazm fort, Portuguese cannon, 1998.

The town of RUSTAQ is located in a huge oasis at the foot of the Hajar Mountains where two *wadi* systems meet, thus controlling access to the mountains. On several occasions during the 17th and 18th centuries, Rustaq was the capital of Oman. It was the base from which the Ya-ruba dynasty ruled before moving to Hazm.

In addition to its political and religious significance, Rustaq has always been, and still is, an important market town.

The fort of Rustaq is an imposing structure and, after Bahla, is the largest fortification in Oman. The original fort dates back to about 600 AD, when the Persians built a castle there. The fort as it stands today was rebuilt when the Ya-ruba Imam Nasir bin Murshid moved his capital from Bahla to Rustaq. In later years, two towers were added.

مدينة الرستاق، ١٩٧٢ وفي الوسط تبدو
القلعة وإلى اليمين بوابة الدخول إلى السوق

The town of Rustaq, 1972. In the centre, the huge fort and, to the right, the entrance gate to the suq.

قلعة الرستاق ١٩٧٢ التي
تعتبر ثاني أكبر قلعة في عمان
بعد قلعة بهلا، ١٩٦٩

The fort of Rustaq, 1972, the largest fortification in Oman after Bahla, 1969.

تقع الرستاق في واحة ضخمة في أسفل جبال الحجر حيث يلتقي واديان مما يجعلها تتحكم في الوصول إلى الجبال. كانت الرستاق في عدة مناسبات خلال القرنين السابع عشر والثامن عشر عاصمة لعمان. وكانت هي القاعدة التي كانت أسرة اليعاربة تحكم منها قبل الانتقال إلى الحزم. وإلى جانب دورها السياسي والديني الكبير ظلت الرستاق ولا تزال مدينة تجارية هامة.

وتأتي قلعة الرستاق الضخمة في المرتبة الثانية بعد قلعة بهلا من حيث الحجم. ويعود تاريخ القلعة الأصلية إلى عام ٦٠٠م حين شيد الفرس حصنا هناك. أما القلعة بشكلها الحالي فقد أعيد بناؤها حين نقل الإمام اليعربي ناصر بن مرشد عاصمته من بهلا إلى الرستاق وأضيف للقلعة خلال السنوات التالية برجا مراقبة.

قلعة الرستاق وسوقها، ١٩٩٩

Rustaq, fort and market, 1999.

قلعة الرستاق بعد ترميمها ١٩٩٩ وتشاهد كابينة الهاتف وسيارة لتعليم السياقة.

The renovated fort at Rustaq, 1999. Note the telephone booth and driving-school car.

صناعة الحلوى في الرستاق، ١٩٧٨

Rustaq, preparing halwa, *1978.*

سوق الخضار والفواكه بالرستاق، ١٩٨٠

Rustaq, fruit and vegetable suq, 1980.

منظر من قلعة الرستاق نحو وادي فار، ١٩٧٣

View from Rustaq fort towards wadi *Far, 1973.*

سوق الخضار بالرستاق
قرب القلعة، ١٩٩٩

Rustaq, vegetable market near fort, 1999.

سوق الرستاق ويبدو من الخلف
مدخل السوق القديم، ١٩٩٩

Rustaq, market, 1999. In the background the entrance to the old suq.

منظر من قلعة الرستاق نحو وادي فار، ١٩٩٩

View from Rustaq fort towards wadi *Far, 1999.*

The town of NAKHL is a quiet village tucked away below the Jebel Nakhl, with the customary fort on a nearby rocky hill. This fort originates from the sixth century, but in its present form, dates back to the 16th century. Because of its strategic position and military strength, the fort played an important role in the history of Oman.

قرية نخل وقلعتها، ١٩٧٨

Nakhl village and fort, 1978.

قلعة نخل، ١٩٧٠

Nakhl fort, 1970.

واحة نخل قرب عيون المياه الحارة ١٩٧٨

Nakhl oasis near the hot water springs, 1978.

تقع مدينة نخل الهادئة في أسفل جبل نخل وتوجد قلعتها فوق تل صخري مجاور. ويعود تاريخ هذه القلعة أصلا إلى القرن السادس إلا أن تاريخها الحديث يعود إلى القرن السادس عشر حيث اتخذت القلعة شكلها الحالي. ولعبت القلعة دورا هاما في تاريخ عمان نظرا لموقعها الاستراتيجي وقوتها العسكرية.

قرية نخل وقلعتها، ٢٠٠٠

Nakhl village and fort, 2000.

قلعة نخل، ٢٠٠٠. كان القوس إلى الشمال من بين العديد من الأقواس التي شيدت بمناسبة زيارة حضرة صاحب الجلالة السلطان قابوس بن سعيد المعظم للولاية خلال احتفالات العيد في يناير ٢٠٠٠

Nakhl fort, 2000. The arch on the left is one of the many decorations erected on the occasion of the visit of HM Sultan Qaboos during the Eid celebrations in January 2000.

سوق نخل، ٢٠٠٠

Nakhl market, 2000.

وادي بني خروص قرب ستال، ١٩٩٩
Wadi *Bani Kharus near Istal, 1999.*

قرية علية في نهاية وادي بني خروص، ١٩٩٩
Ulayh village at the end of wadi *Bani Kharus, 1999*

وادي الهجر قرب السويب، ١٩٩٩
Wadi *Hijir near As Suwayb, 1999.*

وادي مستل قرب مدخل
تجويف الغبرة، ٢٠٠٠

Wadi *Mistal near the entrance to the Ghubrah Bowl, 2000.*

قرية وكان تجثم على التلال في نهاية
تجويف الغبرة، ١٩٧٩

Wakan village perched on the hills at the end of the Ghubrah Bowl, 1979.

Gardens at Wakan village, with the fruit trees in full blossom, 1979. حدائق يانعة الثمار في قرية وكان، ١٩٧٩

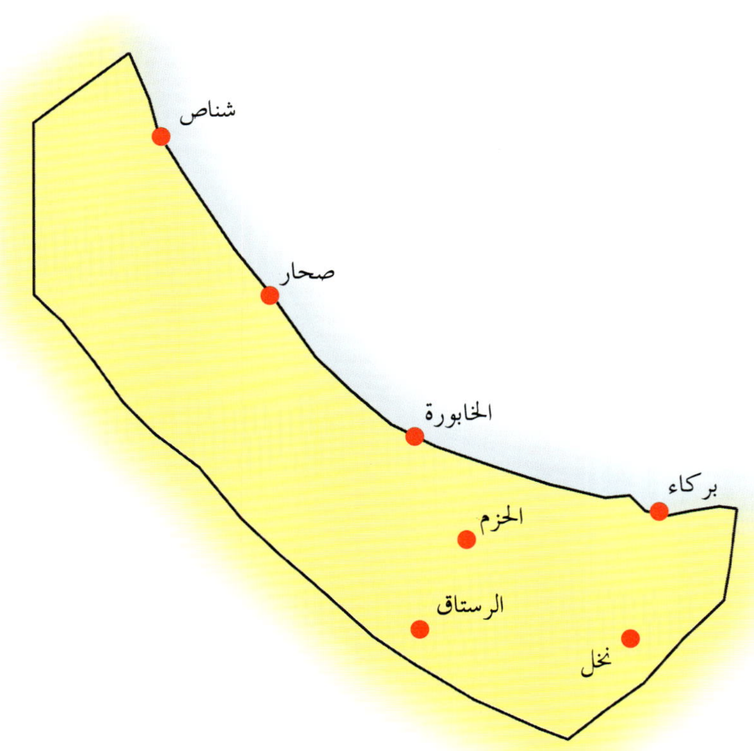

الباطنة

تضم منطقة الباطنة المنطقة الساحلية هلالية الشكل التي تمتد من حدود عمان مع دولة الإمارات في الشمال إلى منتصف المسافة بين مدينتي بركاء والسيب في الجنوب. ويحدها من جهة الشرق خليج عمان فيما يحدها من جهة الغرب الجانب البحري من جبال الحجر الغربي. ولعبت منطقة الباطنة وبخاصة المدن الرئيسية منها وهي صحار وبركاء والرستاق، دورا كبيرا في تاريخ عمان.

إن إحدى المزايا الرئيسية لمنطقة الباطنة هي المياه العذبة التي تأتي من المياه الجوفية الضحلة نسبيا عند جبال الحجر. ونتيجة لذلك تعد معظم أراضي منطقة الباطنة أراضي زراعية خصبة وتزود عمان والدول المجاورة بكميات كبيرة من حاجتها من الفواكه الطازجة (وبخاصة الليمون والتمور) والخضروات والألبان التي دخلت صناعتها إلى المنطقة مؤخرا. وتتمتع منطقة الباطنة أيضا بموقع متميز على بحر يضم أنواعا مختلفة من الأسماك الممتازة. ولكن نظرا لقلة المرافئ على طول الساحل ظلت مهنة صيد الأسماك محدودة على الرغم من وجود مراكب الصيد الحديثة التي حلت محل المراكب التقليدية.

ويقطن في منطقة الباطنة نحو ربع سكان عمان وصحار هي العاصمة.

The Bay and Towns of Muskette and Materen (D. van der Velden 1696).

الخليج ومدينتا مسقط ومطرح (دي. فان دير فيلدن ١٦٩٦)

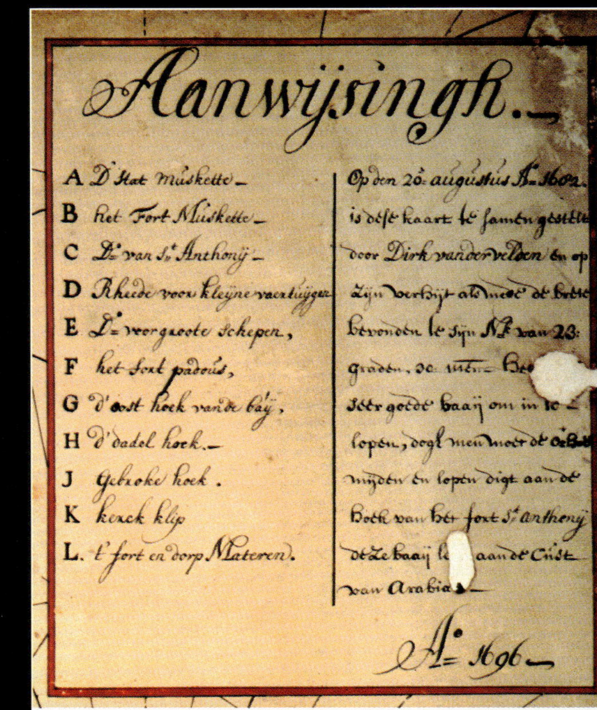

A View of Mutra from the East (R. Temple 1809-1810). منظر لمطرح من الشرق (آر تمبل ١٨٠٩ – ١٨١٠)

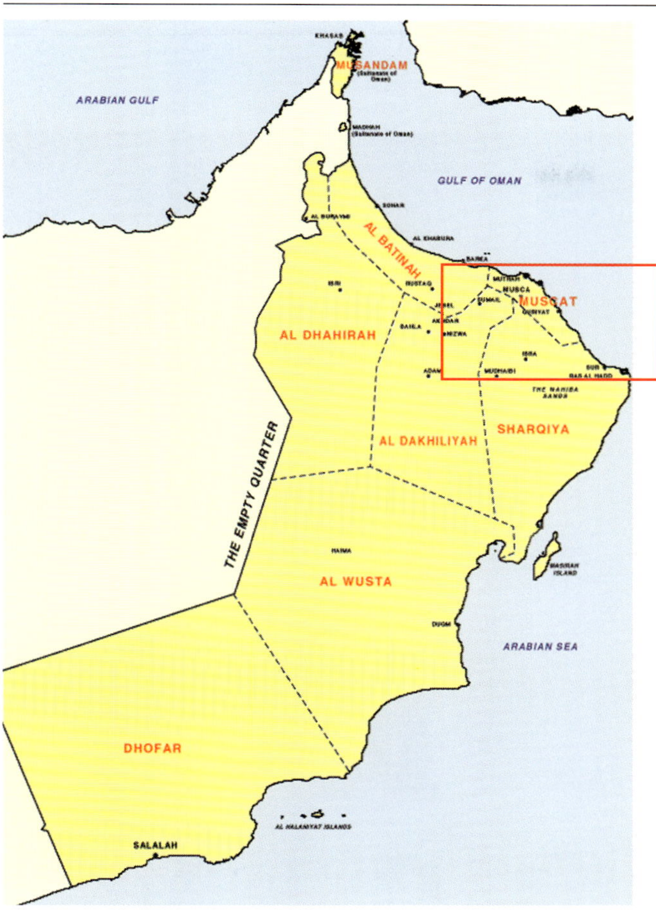

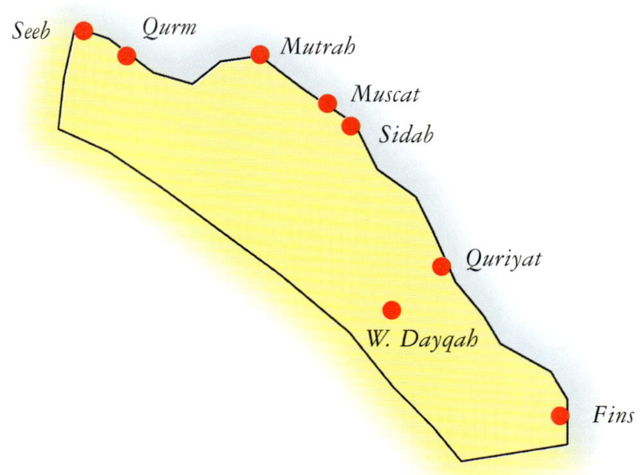

Muscat

The Governate of Muscat comprises a narrow coastal strip in the northeast of the Sultanate of Oman. It extends from the village of Seeb in the northwest to Fins in the southeast, and includes Mutrah, the main port of the country, and the capital Muscat.

Until the early 1970s, activities in this area were very much concentrated on the twin city of Muscat-Mutrah and a few fishing communities and inland villages. However, as wealth, mainly derived from the oil, became available, large-scale building, often in the beautiful Oman-Arab architectural style, has transformed the almost empty area between Mutrah and Seeb into a continuous stretch of prosperous districts linked by modern highways that are bordered by trees and flower beds. These districts, which include Ruwi, Qurm, Medinat Sultan Qaboos, Al Khuweir, Ghubra and Azaiba, house the main businesses, residential areas, and ministries. Approximately one-third of the total population of Oman lives in this area.

مسجد الزلفى بالسيب، ٢٠٠٠

Seeb, Al Zulfa mosque, 2000.

وزارة الإسكان بالخوير، ١٩٩٩

Al Khuweir, Ministry of Housing, 1999.

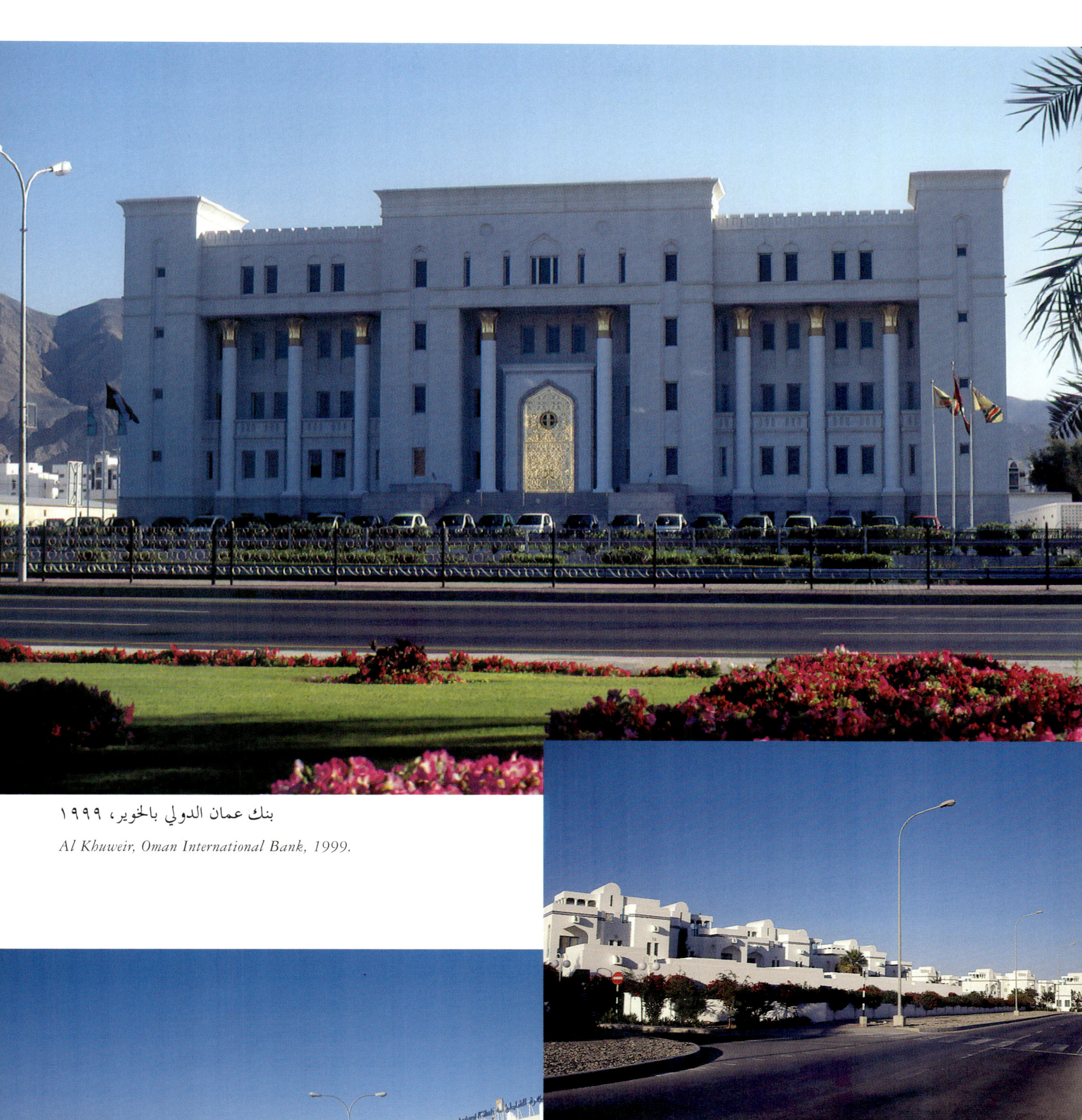

بنك عمان الدولي بالخوير، ١٩٩٩

Al Khuweir, Oman International Bank, 1999.

المنطقة السكنية بمدينة السلطان قابوس، ٢٠٠٠

Medinat Sultan Qaboos, residential area, 2000.

مركز الفير بمدينة السلطان قابوس، ٢٠٠٠

Medinat Sultan Qaboos, Al Fair Square, 2000.

قرية السيب، ١٩٧٤

Seeb village, 1974.

مطار العذيبة، ١٩٧٠

Azaiba Airport, 1970.

مطار السيب الدولي، ١٩٧٣

Seeb International Airport, 1973.

الطريق الرئيسي من السيب إلى ميناء الفحل بعد هطول أمطار غزيرة، ١٩٧٠

Main road from Seeb to Mina Al Fahal after rainstorm, 1970.

Seeb village, 1998. قرية السيب، ١٩٩٨

مطار السيب الدولي، ٢٠٠٠

Seeb International Airport, 2000.

دوار قرب السيب على طريق
صحار مسقط المزدوج، ٢٠٠٠

Roundabout near Seeb on Sohar-Muscat dual carriageway, 2000.

مرتفعات القرم وجزيرة الفحل، ١٩٧٠

Qurm Heights and Fahal island, 1970.

منطقة العذيبة — القرم ١٩٦٥ إلى اليسار جزيرة الفحل وأدنى اليسار مدرج الطائرات في العذيبة.

Azaiba-Qurm area, 1965. Left, Fahal island and below left, the Azaiba airstrip.

الطريق الرئيسي العذيبة-ميناء الفحل (ساحة الصهاريج في الخلف)، ١٩٧٠

Main road Azaiba-Mina Al Fahal (tank farm in the background), 1970.

Qurm Heights and Fahal island, 1998. مرتفعات القرم وجزيرة الفحل، ١٩٩٨

Qurm Heights, 2000 (note tank farm in the centre). مرتفعات القرم ٢٠٠٠ (ساحة الصهاريج في الوسط)

طريق القرم، ١٩٧٠

Qurm road, 1970.

قرية القرم المبنية بسعف النخيل، ١٩٧٠

Qurm barasti *village, 1970.*

قوارب صيد على شاطئ القرم ١٩٧٢ في الخلف المنطقة السكنية لشركة تنمية نفط عمان

Fishing boats on Qurm beach, 1972.

In the background PDO's residential area.

طريق القرم، ٢٠٠٠

Qurm road, 2000.

منطقة القرم السكنية، ١٩٩٩

Qurm, residential area, 1999.

خليج القرم، ٢٠٠٠

Qurm creek, 2000.

First Shell petrol station (Aminda) Qurm, 1973. أول محطة لشل في القرم، ١٩٧٣

المنطقة السكنية والصناعية للشركة، ١٩٧٣

PDO housing and industrial areas, 1973.

المنطقة الصناعية بميناء الفحل ١٩٦٩. إلى اليمين مكاتب الشركة

Mina Al Fahal industrial area, 1969. Right, PDO offices.

محطة شل في القرم، ١٩٩٩

Shell petrol station, Qurm 1999.

المنطقة الصناعية بميناء الفحل، ٢٠٠٠ في الوسط وإلى اليسار مصفاة نفط عمان.

Mina Al Fahal industrial area, 2000. Centre left, the Oman refinery.

مرتفعات القرم من شارع السحمة برأس الحمراء، ١٩٦٦

Panorama of Qurm Heights from Ras Al Hamra-Sahmah Street, 1966.

تقاطع شارع ذياب مع شارع رأس الحمراء ١٩٦٨

View of junction Dhiab and Ras Al Hamra Streets, 1968.

Ras Al Hamra school area, boat and golf clubs, 1974.

مدرسة رأس الحمراء ونادي القوارب ونادي الجولف، ١٩٧٤

ملعب الجولف برأس الحمراء وشارع الفحل ١٩٧٨

Ras Al Hamra golf course and Al Fahal Street, 1978.

مرتفعات القرم من شارع السحمة برأس الحمراء، ١٩٩٩

Panorama of Qurm Heights from Ras Al Hamra-Sahmah Street, 1999.

تقاطع شارع ذياب مع شارع رأس الحمراء، ١٩٩٩

View of junction Dhiab and Ras Al Hamra Streets, 1999.

مدرسة رأس الحمراء ونادي القوارب ونادي الجولف، ١٩٩٩

Ras Al Hamra school area, boat and golf clubs, 1999.

ملعب الجولف برأس الحمراء وشارع الفحل، ١٩٩٩

Ras Al Hamra golf course and Al Fahal Street, 1999.

نقطة الجمارك في روي، ١٩٧٠ (بوابة العشور حدود مسقط وعمان)

Ruwi customs post, 1970 (Al Aushoury Gate; border between Muscat and Oman).

Ruwi village, 1967. قرية روي، ١٩٦٧

Ruwi scene, 1999. Centre left against hill, remains of wall of old border post.

روي، ١٩٩٩ في الوسط وإلى اليسار عند الجبل بقايا جدار نقطة الحدود القديمة.

Ruwi business centre, 2000. Note watchtower in centre.

مركز روي التجاري، ٢٠٠٠ ويظهر برج المراقبة في الوسط

مطار بيت الفلج في منطقة روي. الجمهور بانتظار وصول حضرة صاحب الجلالة السلطان قابوس بن سعيد المعظم في ١٨ أغسطس ١٩٧٠

Bait Al Falaj airport in the Ruwi area. Crowd awaiting the arrival of HM Sultan Qaboos on his visit to the Capital Area, 18 August 1970.

مطار بيت الفلج في الوادي الكبير ١٩٧٢

Ruwi-Bait Al Falaj airport in Wadi *Kabir, 1972.*

قلعة بيت الفلج، القيادة العامة لقوات السلطان المسلحة، ١٩٦٥

Bait Al Falaj fort, headquarters of the SAF (Sultan Armed Forces), 1965.

حلول الظلام على بيت الفلج وروي ومنطقة الوادي الكبير التجارية، ١٩٩٩

*Nightfall over Bait Al Falaj-Ruwi-*Wadi *Kabir business district, 1999.*

قلعة بيت الفلج ومتحف قوات السلطان المسلحة، ١٩٩٩

Bait Al Falaj fort and Sultan Armed Forces Museum, 1999.

Mutrah, located in an equally attractive deep-water bay as Muscat, and also with a Portuguese fort at the eastern end, never gained the same prominence as its neighbour. In part, this may have been due to the fact that Mutrah has fewer surrounding mountains, and was therefore more vulnerable to attacks from inland enemy forces. Nevertheless, Mutrah has always been a significant port and trading centre and, with the modern Mina Sultan Qaboos container port completed in 1974, is today the most important port of the Sultanate. In contrast to Muscat, many of the old buildings and alleyways have been preserved, including the famous suq. Mutrah has the most authentic and extensive suq in the Middle East, with narrow lanes dividing the market into various sectors, each dealing in a particular product, for example, textiles, housewares, gold, silver and spices. Also surviving in Mutrah is the important fish market, now fully modernised.

خليج مطرح من قرية مطيرح، ١٩٦٢

Mutrah bay from Mutairah village, 1962.

بيوت برتغالية في مطرح، ١٩٦٥

Mutrah's Portuguese-style houses, 1965.

Mutrah waterfront, 1969. الواجهة المائية لمطرح ١٩٦٩

كما هو الحال بالنسبة لمسقط تطل مطرح على خليج ساحر عميق المياه كما توجد في طرفها الشرقي قلعة برتغالية إلا أنها لم تنل من الشهرة ما نالتها جارتها . ولعل ذلك يعود إلى قلة الجبال التي تحيط بمطرح مما جعلها أكثر عرضة للهجمات من قوات العدو في الداخل . ومع ذلك ظلت مطرح دائماً ميناءً ومركزاً تجارياً هاماً وبانشاء ميناء السلطان قابوس في عام ١٩٧٤ تعد مطرح اليوم أهم ميناء في السلطنة . ومقارنة مع مسقط أبقت مطرح على العديد من مبانيها وأزقتها القديمة بما فيها سوقها المشهور. ويعد سوق مطرح من أكثر الأسواق وسعاً وعراقة في الشرق الأوسط حيث تنتشر فيها الأزقة الضيقة التي تقسم السوق إلى قطاعات مختلفة يتخصص كل منها في تجارة منتجات محددة كالمنسوجات والأدوات المنزلية والذهبية والفضية والتوابل .

منظر لخليج مطرح من مطيرح، ٢٠٠٠.
تم تشييد العديد من المباني الحديثة وشارع الكورنيش.

Mutrah bay from Mutairah, 2000. Many new buildings have been erected and a corniche now follows the waterfront.

الواجهة المائية لمطرح من سوق السمك، ٢٠٠٠

Mutrah waterfront from the fish market, 2000.

ميناء مطرح، ١٩٧٠

Mutrah harbour, 1970.

ميناء ورصيف مطرح، ١٩٦٢

Mutrah, harbour and jetty, 1962.

سوق السمك في مطرح، ١٩٧٣

Mutrah, fish market, 1973.

ميناء السلطان قابوس بمطرح، ١٩٩٩
وفي المقدمة شارع الكورنيش المزخرف

Mutrah-Mina Sultan Qaboos port, 1999.
Foreground, decorated corniche.

منظر لميناء السلطان قابوس من سوق
السمك، ٢٠٠٠

View of Mutrah-Mina Sultan Qaboos
port from fish market, 2000.

سوق السمك في مطرح، حصيلة اليوم، ١٩٩٩

Mutrah fish market, catch of the day, 1999.

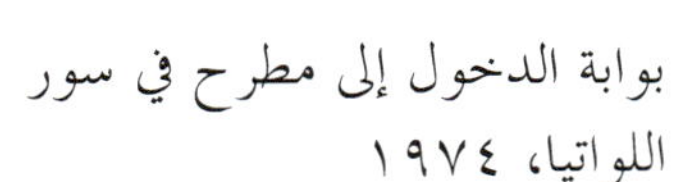

بوابة الدخول إلى مطرح في سور
اللواتيا، ١٩٧٤

Mutrah, entrance gate to the enclosed Lawatiya quarter, 1974.

امرأتان تحملان الماء في مطرح ١٩٥٩ ويظهر
في الخلف سكن الوالي وقلعة مطرح

Mutrah, women carrying water jars, 1959. In the background, the wali*'s residence and Mutrah fort.*

محطة مطرح، ١٩٦٢. المحطة الأخيرة للقوافل القادمة من الداخلية.

Mutrah Terminus, 1962. End station for caravans from the interior.

بوابة الدخول إلى سور اللواتيا بمطرح، ١٩٩٩

Mutrah, entrance gate to the Lawatiya quarter, 1999.

قلعة مطرح ومناطق الخور الجديدة، ١٩٩٩

Mutrah fort and modern Al Khour quarters, 1999.

مركز شرطة مطرح وموقف سيارات الأجرة، ٢٠٠٠

Mutrah police station and taxi stand, 2000.

مدخل ومخرج سوق مطرح من جهة البحر ١٩٦٢

Mutrah suq, seaside entrance/exit, 1962.

أحد زقاق التسوق العديدة بسوق مطرح ١٩٧٠

Mutrah suq, one of the many shopping alleys, 1970.

مدخل ومخرج سوق مطرح، ١٩٦٢

Mutrah suq entrance/exit, 1962.

مدخل/مخرج سوق مطرح من جهة البحر، ٢٠٠٠
Mutraq suq, seaside entrance/exit, 2000.

شارع التسوق الرئيسي بسوق مطرح، ٢٠٠٠
Mutraq suq, main shopping street, 2000.

مدخل/مخرج سوق مطرح من جهة المدينة، ١٩٩٩
Mutraq suq, townside entrance/exit, 1999.

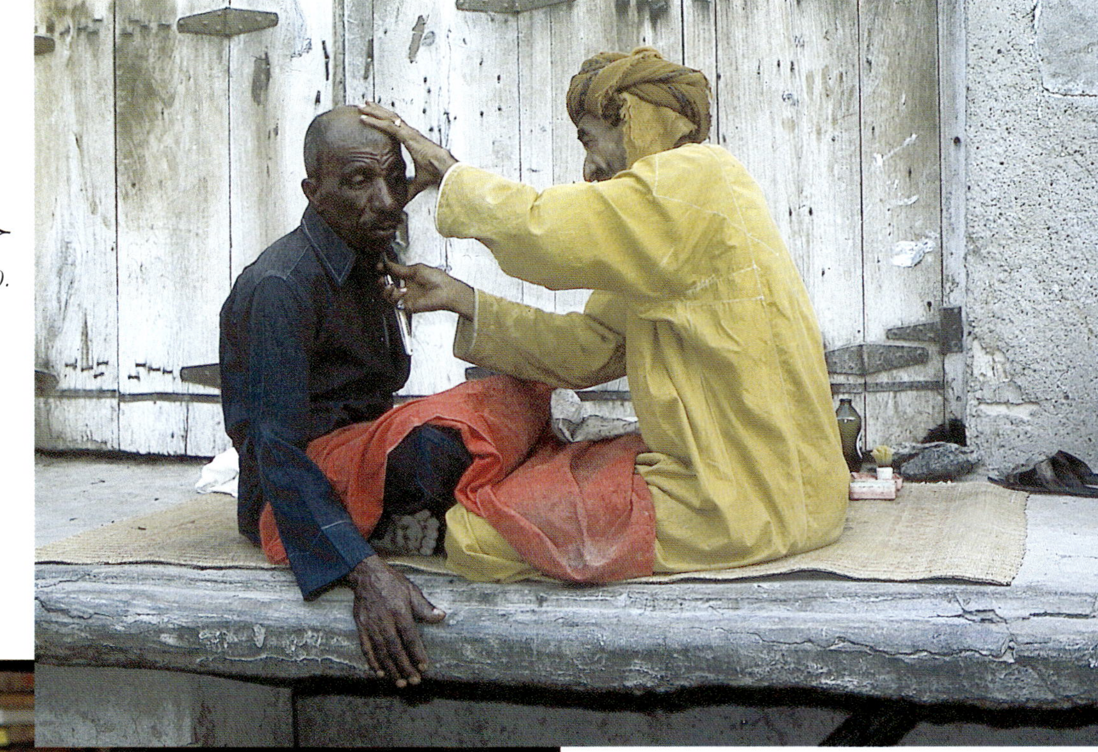

حلاق منهمك في عمله، ١٩٧٠

Barber at work, 1970.

مكتبة، ١٩٧٣

Bookshop, 1973.

صناعة البنادق، ١٩٧٢

Gunsmith, 1972.

Mutrah, antique and curio shop, 2000. متجر لبيع التحف بمطرح، ٢٠٠٠

قرية ريام وخليج مطرح
١٩٦٢، التقطت من عقبة ريام

Riyam village and Mutrah bay, 1962, taken from Aqbat Riyam.

MUSCAT, well protected by a ring of mountains, has a beautiful natural deep-water harbour. First described in the ninth century, Muscat only started to gain wider recognition in the 14th and 15th centuries when it slowly emerged from the dominance of Hormuz. In the early 16th century, attracted by its favourable location for trade with India, the Portuguese, under Alfonso d'Albuquerque, developed Muscat as their principal base. They strengthened the defences with large walls and two great forts. The western fort, Mirani, was completed in 1587 and the eastern fort, Jalali, in 1588. Despite these defences, by 1650, Omani forces under Imam Sultan bin Saif had already ousted the Portuguese. During the following period under Ya'ruba rule, trade flourished and the city of Muscat was modernised and expanded. In 1779, Imam Ahmad bin Said, founder of the dynasty still in power today, made Muscat his capital, but in 1828, Sultan Said bin Sultan transferred the seat of government to Zanzibar. After the loss of Zanzibar in 1861, the fortunes of Muscat rapidly declined, and it was not until 1970 when HM Sultan Qaboos took over that large-scale renovations were carried out, making Muscat the prominent capital it is today.

منظر لمسقط من قمة عقبة ريام
١٩٦٧. ويمكن مشاهدة قلعتي
الميراني والجلالي

View of Muscat from the top of Aqbat Riyam, 1967. Mirani and Jalali forts can be seen rising out of the late afternoon clouds.

قرية ريام وخليج مطرح وميناء السلطان قابوس، ٢٠٠٠

Riyam village, Mutrah bay and the newly built Mina Sultan Qaboos port, 2000.

تتميز مسقط بمرفأ طبيعي ساحر عميق المياه تحميه سلسلة من الجبال. ومع ان ذكرها ورد لأول مرة في القرن التاسع إلا أن مسقط بدأت تكتسب اهتماماً أكبر خلال القرنين الرابع عشر والخامس عشر مع خروجها من سيطرة هرمز . وقام البرتغاليون في بداية القرن السادس عشر بقيادة ألفونسو ألبوكيرك بتطوير مسقط كقاعدتهم الرئيسية وذلك بفضل موقعها المتميز للتجارة مع الهند. فقاموا بتعزيز دفاعاتهم بتشييد جدران كبيرة وقلعتين عظيمتين . واكتمل بناء القلعة الغربية المعروفة باسم الميراني في ١٥٨٧ في حين اكتملت القلعة الشرقية المعروفة بقلعة الجلالي في ١٥٨٨ . ولكن وعلى الرغم من هذه الدفاعات تمكنت القوات العمانية بقيادة الإمام سلطان بن سيف من طرد البرتغاليين في ١٦٥٠. وخلال فترة حكم اليعاربة التي تلت ازدهرت التجارة وتوسعت مسقط وصارت مدينة حديثة . في عام ١٧٧٩ اتخذ الإمام احمد بن سعيد مؤسس الأسرة المالكة الكريمة من مسقط عاصمة له ، إلا أن السلطان سعيد بن سلطان قام بتحويل كرسي الحكم إلى زنجبار في ١٨٢٨ . وبعد فقدان السيطرة على زنجبار عام ١٨٦١ تضاءلت ثروات مسقط بسرعة و لم تستعد مسقط رونقها إلا في عام ١٩٧٠ حين تقلد حضرة صاحب الجلالة السلطان قابوس بن سعيد زمام الحكم في البلاد حيث شهدت مسقط تطوراً شاملاً جعلها تستعيد مكانتها عاصمة للسلطنة .

منظر لمدينة مسقط، ٢٠٠٠. يمكن مشاهدة العديد من المباني الجديدة بما في ذلك قصر العلم في الوسط.

Scenic view of Muscat, 2000. Many new buildings, including the Al Alam palace in the centre, are visible.

تم تزيين الباب الكبير بمسقط بمناسبة الزيارة الأولى التي تفضل بها حضرة صاحب الجلالة السلطان قابوس بن سعيد المعظم لمنطقة العاصمة في ١٨ أغسطس ١٩٧٠

Muscat, Bab Al Kabir gate, decorated for HM Sultan Qaboos' first visit to the Capital Area on 18 August, 1970.

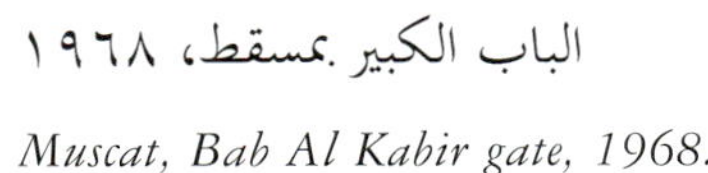

الباب الكبير بمسقط، ١٩٦٨

Muscat, Bab Al Kabir gate, 1968.

الباب الكبير بمسقط، ١٩٧٢ هذه هي البوابة الرئيسية والوحيدة التي تسمح للسيارات بدخول المدينة.

Muscat, Bab Al Kabir gate, 1972. This was the main gate and the only one that allowed vehicles to enter the city.

الباب الكبير بمسقط من داخل المدينة المسورة، ١٩٧٣

Muscat, Bab Al Kabir gate from within the walled town, 1973.

Muscat, the redesigned Bab Al Kabir gate, 1999. الباب الكبير الذي اعيد تصميمه ١٩٩٩

Muscat, Bab Al Kabir gate from inside the town, 2000. الباب الكبير من داخل المدينة، ٢٠٠٠

مسجد الخور بمسقط، التقطت من قلعة الميراني، ١٩٧٠

Muscat, Khor mosque taken from Mirani fort, 1970.

باب المثعاب بمسقط، التقطت من قلعة الميراني، ١٩٧٠

Muscat, Bab Mithaib gate taken from Mirani fort, 1970.

مسجد الخور وقلعة الميراني بمسقط
١٩٦٢. إلى اليسار بيت جريزا

Muscat, Khor mosque and Mirani fort, 1962. On the left, Bait Graiza house.

قلعة الميراني بمسقط، ١٩٧٣

Muscat, Mirani fort, 1973.

مسجد الخور بمسقط، التقطت من قلعة الميراني، ٢٠٠٠

Muscat, Khor mosque taken from Mirani fort, 2000.

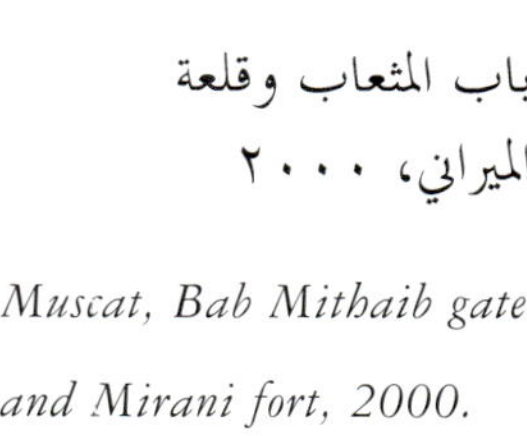

باب المثعاب وقلعة الميراني، ٢٠٠٠

Muscat, Bab Mithaib gate and Mirani fort, 2000.

مسجد الخور وقلعة الميراني، ٢٠٠٠
إلى اليسار بيت جريزا

Muscat, Khor mosque and Mirani fort, 2000. On the left, Bait Graiza house.

قلعة الميراني بمسقط، ١٩٩٩

Muscat, Mirani fort, 1999.

قلعة الجلالي بمسقط، ١٩٧٣

Muscat, Jalali fort, 1973.

رصيف وميناء الخور بمسقط، ١٩٧٠ إلى اليمين قصر العلم القديم

Muscat, Khor jetty and harbour front, 1970. On the right, the old Al Alam palace.

رصيف الخور بمسقط وقلعة الجلالي ١٩٦٩

Muscat, Khor jetty and Jalali fort, 1969.

Muscat, Jalali fort, 1996. قلعة الجلالي .بمسقط، ١٩٩٦

Muscat, view of new Al Alam Palace and Jalali fort, 2000. منظر لقصر العلم الجديد وقلعة الجلالي، ٢٠٠٠

حارسان على مدخل قصر العلم القديم، ١٩٦٦

Muscat, guards at the entrance to the old Al Alam Palace, 1966.

مسجد الزواوي بمسقط، ١٩٧٣

Muscat, Zawawi mosque, 1973.

Sidab, vista of Sultan Turki Street, 1973. منظر لسداب من شارع السلطان تركي، ١٩٧٣

بوابة الدخول إلى قصر العلم، ٢٠٠٠

Muscat, entrance gate to Al Alam Palace, 2000.

مسجد الزواوي بمسقط، ١٩٩٩

Muscat, Zawawi mosque, 1999.

منظر لسداب من شارع السلطان تركي، ١٩٩٩

Sidab, view of Sultan Turki Street, 1999.

QURIYAT is located on a wide flat bay, surrounded by date groves, some 85 km southeast of Muscat. Like many coastal towns in Oman, Quriyat was ransacked during the Portuguese campaign under Albuquerque, and its inhabitants massacred. A lone watchtower on a rocky cliff at the edge of the harbour is all that remains of the Portuguese occupation. In those days, horse breeding was a major activity in the area, but this did not survive. Instead, Quriyat, boasting some of the richest fishing grounds nearby, has developed into an important fishing centre with a modern port and market facilities.

قارب صيد قديم في قريات، ويظهر في الخلف برج مراقبة برتغالي، ١٩٧٤

Quriyat, antique fishing boat with old Portuguese watchtower in the background, 1974.

صيادون من قريات على الساحل، ١٩٧٣

Quriyat, fishermen on the beach, 1973.

تقع قريات على بعد ٨٥ كليومتراً جنوب شرقي مسقط وتطل على خليج واسع وتحف بها أشجار النخيل من كل جانب. وتعرضت قريات شأنها شأن العديد من المدن الساحلية إلى الدمار ابان الحملة البرتغالية بقيادة ألبوكيرك وقتل سكانها. ويوجد برج للمراقبة فوق تل صخري في نهاية المرفأ وهو كل ما تبقى من آثار الاحتلال البرتغالي. وكانت تربية الجياد هي النشاط الرئيسي في المنطقة إلا أنها لم تستمر . ويعد صيد الأسماك الآن هو النشاط الرئيسى في قريات التي تطورت إلى مركز هام لصيد الأسماك مجهز بمرفأ ومرافق تسويق حديثة .

قوارب الصيد الحديثة في قريات وبرج المراقبة البرتغالي القديم، ١٩٩٩

Quriyat, modern fishing boats and old Portuguese watchtower, 1999.

قرية قريات، ١٩٩٩

Quriyat, village, 1999.

Bandar Jissah near Muscat, calm waters, numerous coves and secluded beaches, 1995.

بندر الجصة قرب مسقط. مياه هادئة
وكهوف كثيرة وشواطئ منعزلة، ١٩٩٥

Khayran fishing village about 10 km from Yiti, 2000.

قرية خيران التي يعمل أهلها بالصيد وتبعد حوالي ١٠كم من يتي، ٢٠٠٠

Wadi *Dayqah in the Eastern Hajar, 1979.* وادي ضيقة على جبال الحجر الشرقي، ١٩٧٩

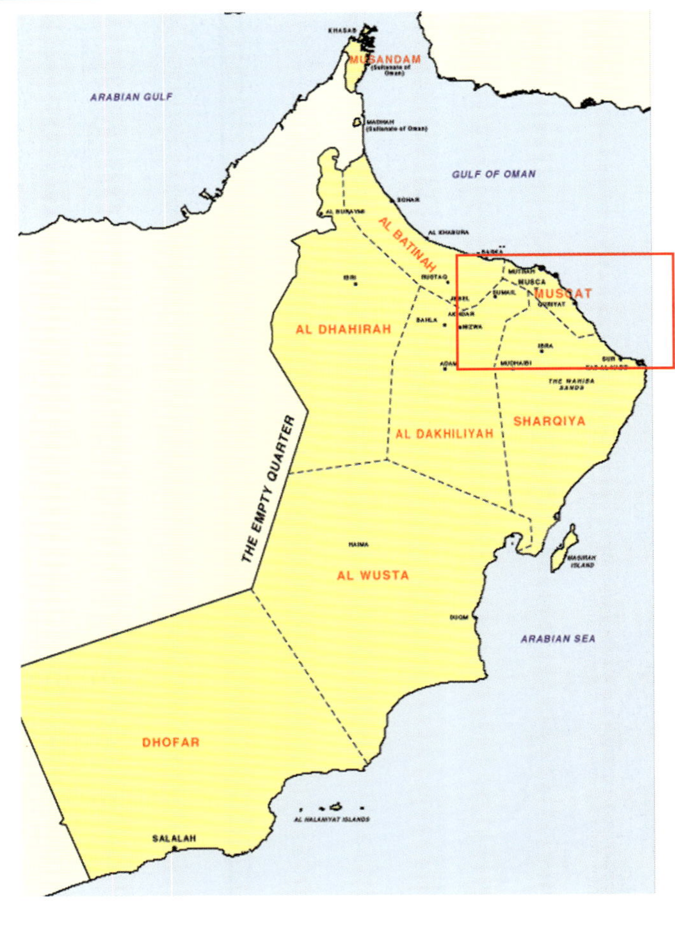

مسقط

تضم محافظة مسقط شريطا ساحليا ضيقا في شمال شرقي السلطنة يمتد من قرية السيب في الشمال الغربي إلى فنس في الجنوب الشرقي ويضم مدينة مطرح وهي الميناء الرئيسي في البلاد ومسقط العاصمة . وكانت الأنشطة في هذه المنطقة حتى بداية السبعينيات تتمركز في مدينتي مسقط و مطرح وبعض قرى الصيد في الداخل. على انه ونتيجة للثروة التي تحققت بشكل رئيسي من النفط ظهرت إلى الوجود مبان شاهقة شيدت على طراز المعمار العماني الاسلامي الجميل جعلت من المنطقة شبه الخالية من العمران والممتدة من السيب إلى مطرح أحياء سكنية راقية تربط بعضها ببعض طرق حديثة تحف بها الأشجار والزهور وتضم هذه الأحياء روي والقرم ومدينة السلطان قابوس والخوير والغبرة والعذيبة وتوجد فيها الوزارات وتنتشر فيها المحلات التجارية والمناطق السكنية . ويقطن في هذه المنطقة حوالي ثلث سكان السلطنة .

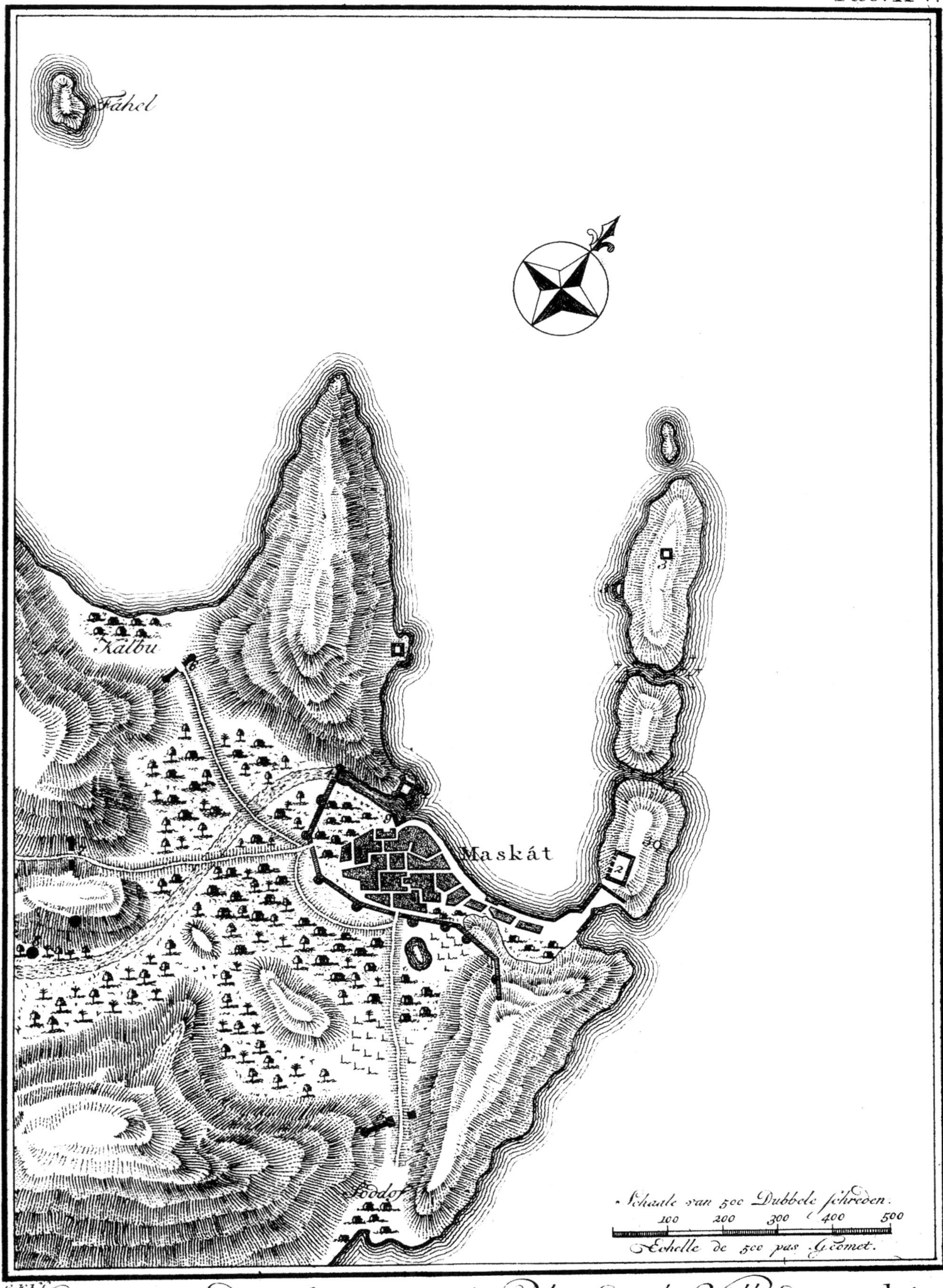

Grondtekening der Stad Maskát. ‖ Plan de la Ville de Maskát.

City plan of Maskát (C. Niebuhr-1774). مخطط مدينة مسقط (سي. نيبوهار ١٧٧٤)

The Forts of Jellali & Merani, Muskat (W. Daniells-1793).

قلعتا الجلالي والميراني بمسقط (دبليو. دانالز ١٧٩٣)

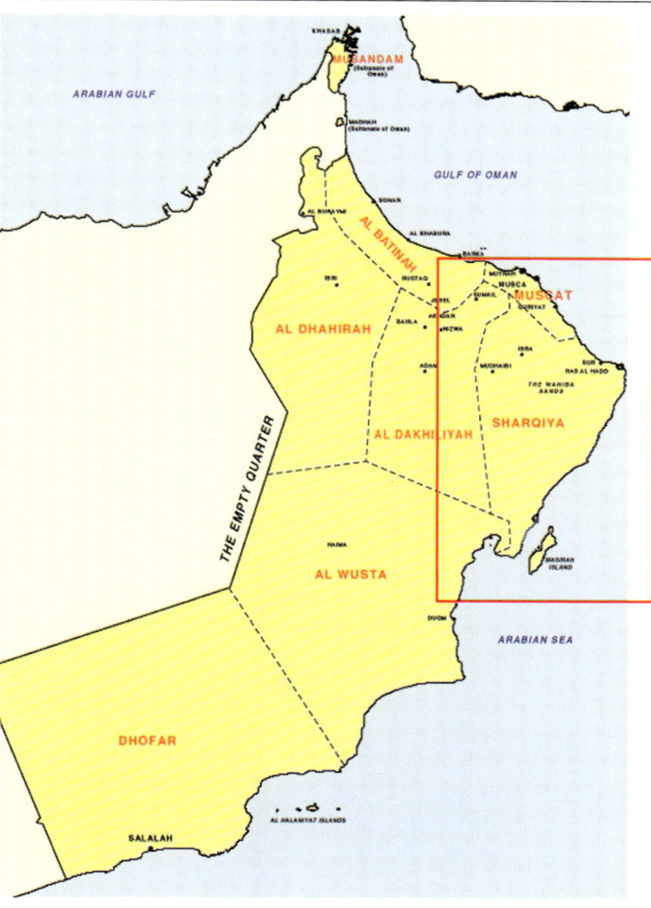

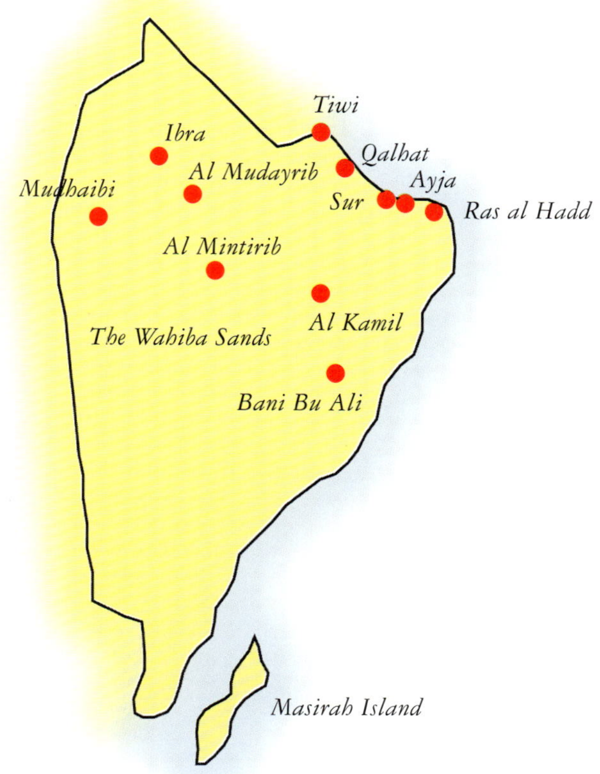

Sharqiya

The Sharqiya province is located to the east of the *wadi* Semail, a major 'divide' that splits the Hajar Mountains into a western and an eastern range. Along the coast, the Sharqiya stretches from Tiwi in the east via Ras al Hadd to Masirah Island in the southeast. Inland, it includes the eastern Hajar Mountains with several large *wadi* systems (Shab, Tiwi, Tayin and Bani Khalid) and the Wahiba, an ancient wedge-shaped sand-sea. The principal town is Sur, historically the main gateway from Oman to its African colonies. Major towns in the interior include Bilad Bani Bu Ali and Al Mintirib on the edge of the Wahiba Sands, and Al Mudayrib and Ibra on the lower plains of the Hajar Mountains. The Sharqiya area is inhabited by a large number of tribes who, at various times, have played a prominent role in the history of Oman.

Al Qabil area, sunrise in the Eastern Hajar, 1999.

شروق الشمس على جبال الحجر الشرقي في منطقة القابل، ١٩٩٩

مصب وادي شعب
قرب طيوي، ١٩٧٨

Mouth of the wadi *Shab near Tiwi, 1978.*

Wadi *Tayin after heavy rain, 1982.* وادي الطائيين بعد هطول أمطار غزيرة، ١٩٨٢

منظر عام لوادي
طيوي، ١٩٦٨

Scenic view of the wadi *Tiwi, 1968.*

طيوي على ضفاف وادي شعب، ١٩٧٦

Tiwi on the banks of the wadi *Shab, 1976.*

تقع طيوي على الساحل في أرض خصبة كثيرة المياه بين واديي شعب وطيوي . وطيوي من المدن القديمة ووصفها الرحالة العربي ابن بطوطة في القرن الرابع عشر عندما زار مدينة قلهات القريبة منها. وتشتهر طيوي بإنتاج أنواع ممتازة من الفواكه والأسماك

TIWI is located on the coast in a fertile, well-watered area between the *wadi*s Shab and Tiwi. It is an ancient town, described by the 14th century Arabian traveller Ibn Battuta when he visited nearby Qalhat. Tiwi has always been known as a producer of excellent fruit and fish.

Tiwi, outlook from the mountains, 1967.

منظر عام لطيوي من الجبال، ١٩٦٧

Tiwi, view from the mountains, 2000.

منظر عام لطيوي من الجبال، ٢٠٠٠

طيوي على ضفاف وادي شاب، ١٩٩٩

Tiwi on the banks of the wadi *Shab, 1999.*

ضريح بيبي مريم في قلهات، ١٩٧٠

Qalhat, the Bibi Miriam tomb, 1970.

الزخرفة داخل ضريح بيبي
مريم بقلهات، ١٩٧٠

Qalhat, decorations inside the Bibi Miriam tomb, 1970.

The town of QALHAT lying halfway between Tiwi and Sur, is believed to have been founded by the Persians (Sassanid period). In the second century AD it became the seat of government of the Azdites, following their migration from Yemen. The city reached the height of its prosperity as the most important port on the Arabian coast in the 13th-14th centuries under the rule of Hormuz. During this period, Marco Polo and, later, Ibn Battuta visited Qalhat, and both were favourably impressed by its beauty. Fortunes, however, declined as Qalhat was first damaged by an earthquake and thereafter sacked by the Portuguese in 1508. Now only scant ruins remain.

جدران المدينة الخارجية ومصنع الغاز الطبيعي المسال الجديدة في قلهات، ٢٠٠٠

Qalhat, remains of the outer city walls and new LNG plant, 2000.

أطلال قلهات، ٢٠٠٠

Qalhat, view of the ruins, 2000.

الزخرفة داخل ضريح بيبي مريم بقلهات، ٢٠٠٠

Qalhat, decorations inside the Bibi Miriam tomb, 2000.

تقع مدينة قلهات في منتصف المسافة بين طيوي وصور ويعتقد أن الفرس هم الذين أنشأوها (في عصر الساسانيين). وأصبحت في القرن الثاني الميلادي مقر الحكم للأزديين بعد هجرتهم من اليمن . وبلغت المدينة أوج عظمتها كأهم ميناء على الساحل العربي خلال القرنين الثالث والرابع عشر إبان فترة حكم الملك هرمز. وزارها خلال هذه الفترة ماركو بولو ومن بعده ابن بطوطة وأعجب كلاهما بجمالها . وبدأت ثروات قلهات تتضاءل بعد تعرضها أولا لهزة أرضية ليعقبها الغزو البرتغالي في عام ١٥٠٨ . ولم يتبق من المدينة الآن سوى أطلال متناثرة هنا وهناك .

Ayja at the mouth of the Khor al Batha creek, 1976. العيجة على مدخل خور البطحاء، ١٩٧٦

Ayja bay, 1976. خليج العيجة، ١٩٧٦

غروب الشمس بصور، ١٩٧٠
Sunset at Sur, 1970.

SUR and its twin city AYJA just across the lagoon are ancient settlements with a sheltered bay and a long creek providing a natural harbour. Left untouched by the Portuguese and with the *wadi* Falayi as an easy route into the Interior, Sur developed as the main trading port of Oman with India and East Africa. Although overtaken by the better shipping facilities in Mutrah in recent years, Sur is still an important port and fish market, and is the only place left in Oman with active dhow (*sambuq* type) building yards. Modern housing and port facilities, together with the recently opened LNG plant, have given Sur a new lease of life.

خليج العيجة، ٢٠٠٠ *Ayja bay, 2000.*

العيجة على مدخل خور البطحاء، ١٩٩٩

Ayja at the mouth of the Khor al Batha creek, 1999.

تعتبر مدينتا صور والعيجة التي تقع على الضفة الأخرى للخليج من المستوطنات القديمة ويتيح خليجها المحمي الطويل مرفأ طبيعيا. وحيث أن يد البرتغاليين لم تطلها ومع وجود وادي الفليج كطريق سهل للمناطق الداخلية، تطورت صور كميناء رئيسي للتجارة مع الهند وشرق أفريقيا.

ومازالت صور تشكل ميناء مهما وسوقا للسمك على الرغم من أن مرافق التحميل الأفضل بمطرح سرقت منها الأضواء. وهي المكان الوحيد في عمان الذي يوجد به ساحة لصناعة سفن الغنجة (سمبوك) التقليدية.
أعطت البيوت الجديدة ومرافق الميناء ومصنع الغاز الطبيعي المسال الذي افتتح مؤخرا وهجا جديدا لمدينة صور.

غروب الشمس في الخليج، ٢٠٠٠

Sur, sunset on the creek, 2000.

الواجهة المائية لصور، ١٩٧٢

Sur, water front, 1972.

شارع ومسجد في صور، ١٩٧٢

Sur, street and mosque, 1972.

ساحة الغنجة ومسجد في صور، ١٩٧٢

Sur, dhow yard and mosque, 1972.

الواجهة المائية لصور، ١٩٩٩

Sur, water front, 1999.

منظر عام من جبل العيجة، ٢٠٠٠. إلى اليسار يمكن مشاهدة عدة ساحات لصناعة قوارب الغنجة

Sur, view from the hill at Ayja, 2000. To the left, several dhow building yards can be seen.

الجامع الكبير في صور، ٢٠٠٠

Sur, the Grand Mosque, 2000.

صناعة الغنجة في صور، ١٩٧٢

Sur, building a dhow (sambuq), *1972.*

سفينة سنبك بصور، ١٩٧٣

Sur, sambuq *at anchor, 1973.*

إنزال المسافرين في صور، ١٩٧٢

Sur, unloading passengers, 1972.

محل صناعة السنابك وصيانتها، ١٩٩٨

Sur, sambuq *building and repair shop, 1998.*

بيع السمك في خليج صور، ١٩٩٨

Sur creek, fish auction, 1998.

إنزال المسافرين في صور، ١٩٩٩

Sur, unloading passengers, 1999.

Sur, mending nets, 1973. إصلاح شباك الصيد في صور، ١٩٧٣

RAS AL HADD is the most easterly point of Oman and the Arabian Peninsula. It comprises a sandy beach, a village and a fort, but is better known for the world's largest concentration of green turtles. Nearby are the remains of an airfield, used by the British as a staging post during World War II.

Ras Al Hadd fort, 1976. قلعة رأس الحد، ١٩٧٦

Sur, mending nets, on the left the new corniche, 2000. إصلاح شباك الصيد وشارع الكورنيش الجديد إلى اليسار، ٢٠٠٠

رأس الحد هي أقصى نقطة شرقية لعمان وشبه الجزيرة العربية. وتشمل ساحلا رمليا وقرية وقلعة ولكنها معروفة بتواجد أكبر عدد من السلاحف الخضراء فيها على مستوى العالم. ويقع قربها بقايا مهبط طائرات استخدمه البريطانيون كمنطقة لتجميع قواتهم العسكرية خلال الحرب العالمية الثانية.

Ras Al Hadd fort, 1999. قلعة رأس الحد، ١٩٩٩

طيوي على ضفاف وادي شاب، ١٩٩٩

Bilad Sur, Eid Al Adha market, 1968.

سوق بلاد صور، ١٩٦٨

Bilad Sur, market, 1968.

سباق الهجن بمناسبة عيد الأضحى
في بلاد صور، ١٩٦٨

Bilad Sur, camel races, Eid Al Adha, 1968.

سوق بلاد صور وقلعتها، ١٩٩٩

Bilad Sur, market square and fort, 1999.

Bilad Sur, fort, 2000. قلعة بلاد صور، ٢٠٠٠

أحد رجال القبيلة من بلاد صور، ١٩٦٨ *Bilad Sur, tribesman, 1968.*

فتاة من صور، ١٩٧٣

Sur, girl, 1973.

فتاتان من القابل، ١٩٧٢

Al Qabil, girls, 1972.

شاب من الكامل، ١٩٩٩

Al Kamil, young boy, 1999.

Al Mintirib, Beduin woman, 1998. بدوية من المنتدرب ١٩٩٨

Al Kamil is strategically located approximately 60 km from Sur, near the Wahiba Sands where the *wadi*s Falahi and al Batha meet, the former leading to Sur and the latter to Bilad Bani Bu Ali. Al Kamil has an active market near the old fort.

Al Kamil, view of the town, 1972.   منظر عام لمدينة الكامل، ١٩٧٢

Al Kamil, market square, 1972.   سوق الكامل، ١٩٧٢

تحتل مدينة الكامل موقعا استراتيجيا على بعد نحو ٦٠ كيلومترا من صور وبالقرب من رمال
آل وهيبة حيث يلتقي واديا الفلاحي وبطحاء حيث يتجه الأول إلى صور فيما ينحدر الثاني
نحو بلاد بني بوعلي. ويوجد في الكامل سوق ذو حركة تجارية نشطة بالقرب من القلعة القديمة .

Al Kamil, scene of the Thursday market, 1999. سوق الخميس في القابل، ١٩٩٩

Al Kamil, Beduin woman selling embroidery, 1999. بدوية تبيع مشغولات مطرزة في الكامل، ١٩٩٩

Al Kamil, market, 1999. سوق الكامل، ١٩٩٩

Al Mintirib and Al Qabil, the latter being the old capital of the region, are located amid extensive palm groves and gardens on the edge of the Wahiba Sands. Both are typical desert towns suffering from the encroachment of the desert sands. Beduin living on the fringes of the Wahiba meet and sell their produce at the towns.

Al Qabil and the Wahiba Sands, 1970. القابل ورمال آل وهيبة، ١٩٧٠

زحف الرمال قرب المنترب، ١٩٧٨

Encroachment of sand near Al Mintirib, 1978.

Transport in the Wahiba Sands, 1970. وسائل النقل في رمال آل وهيبة، ١٩٧٠

تقع مدينة المنترب والقابل - والأخيرة هي العاصمة القديمة للمنطقة - وسط مزارع واسعة من النخيل والحدائق الشاسعة على أطراف رمال آل وهيبة. وتعتبر المدينتان نموذجا للمدن الصحراوية التي تعاني من الزحف الصحراوي . وتلتقى القبائل البدوية التي تقطن في حواف رمال آل وهيبة في المدينتين لبيع منتجاتهم .

Al Qabil, old and new along the Wahiba Sands, 1999.

اجتمع الماضي والحاضر معا في القابل على طول رمال آل وهيبة، ١٩٩٩

المنترب، وسائل النقل في رمال آل وهيبة، ١٩٩٩

Al Mintirib, transport near the Wahiba Sands, 1999.

Al Mudayrib, lying some 20 km south of Ibra, is relatively young by Omani standards. Founded in the 18th century, the town is characterised by a large number of watchtowers, not only on the surrounding hilltops but also alongside houses, fortified mansions and town walls. Al Mudayrib is a very pleasant town, probably because it has been able to preserve its typical character, successfully blending the old and the new.

Al Mudayrib, view from the north, 1970.   منظر عام للمضيرب من الشمال، ١٩٧٠

منظر عام للمضيرب من الشمال الغربي، ١٩٧٨

Al Mudayrib, view from the northwest, 1978.

Al Mudayrib, view from the south, 1978.   منظر عام للمضيرب من الجنوب، ١٩٧٨

تعد المضيرب ، التي تقع جنوبي ابراء بنحو ٢٠ كيلومترا ، مدينة حديثة نسبيا بالمعايير العمانية . وتأسست المدينة في القرن الثامن عشر وتتميز بكثرة أبراج المراقبة فيها ليس فقط على قمم التلال المحيطة وإنما وسط الأحياء السكنية والمباني المحصنة وعلى أسوار المدينة . والمضيرب مدينة رائعة وقد تعزى روعتها إلى قدرة المدينة على الحفاظ على نسيج رائع من القديم والحديث .

منظر عام للمضيرب من الشمال، ٢٠٠٠

Al Mudayrib, view from the north, 2000.

Al Mudayrib, outlook from the south, 1999.

منظر عام للمضيرب من الجنوب، ١٩٩٩

Al Mudayrib, market street, 1978. شارع سوق المضيرب، ١٩٧٨

سوق المضيرب،
١٩٧٨

Al Mudayrib, market square, 1978.

شارع سوق المضيرب، ١٩٩٩

Al Mudayrib, market street, 1999.

باب منحوت ببراعة، ١٩٩٩

Al Mudayrib, beautifully carved doors, 1999.

سوق المضيرب، ١٩٩٦

Al Mudayrib, market, 1996.

IBRA is the largest, and it is also believed to be the oldest, town of the Sharqiya. The centre is characterised by many substantial and beautifully decorated houses dating back to the 19th century, when trade with East Africa was at its peak. Most have now been deserted as a modern town has developed outside the old city walls.

بيت تقليدي لأسرة من القرن التاسع عشر الميلادي، ١٩٧٦

Ibra, traditional 19th century family home, 1976.

Shell petrol station in the Sharqiya, 1973. محطة شل بالشرقية، ١٩٧٣

ابراء هي أكبر مدينة في المنطقة الشرقية ويعتقد أنها الأقدم . وتتوسط المدينة مساكن رائعة الجمال يعود تاريخها إلى القرن التاسع عشر حين كانت التجارة مع شرق أفريقيا في أوج ازدهارها . غير أن معظم هذه المساكن هجرها أهلها إلى مدينة حديثة شيدت خارج أسوار المدينة القديمة .

Ibra, panorama of the old and new town, 2000. منظر للمدينة القديمة والحديثة، ٢٠٠٠

Shell petrol station, 2000. محطة شل، ٢٠٠٠

Wahiba Sands near Al Qabil, 1996. رمال آل وهيبة قرب القابل، ١٩٩٦

In the Wahiba Sands, 1997. على رمال آل وهيبة، ١٩٩٧

مسجد آل حمودة في بلاد بني بوعلي، ١٩٩٩

Bilad Banu Bu Ali, Al Hamoodah mosque, 1999.

White beaches on Masirah Island, 1997. سواحل بيضاء في جزيرة مصيرة، ١٩٩٧

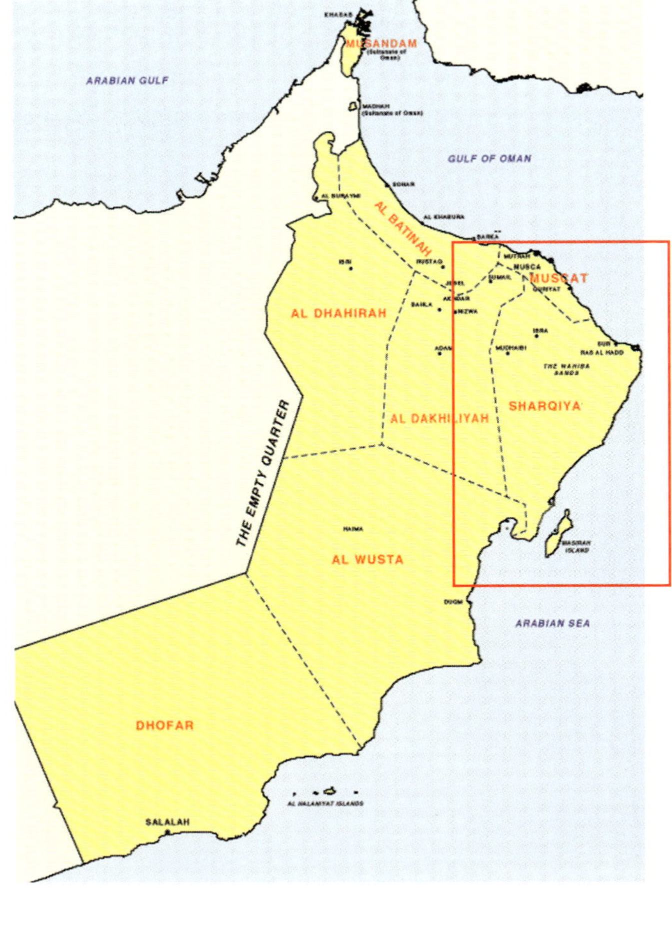

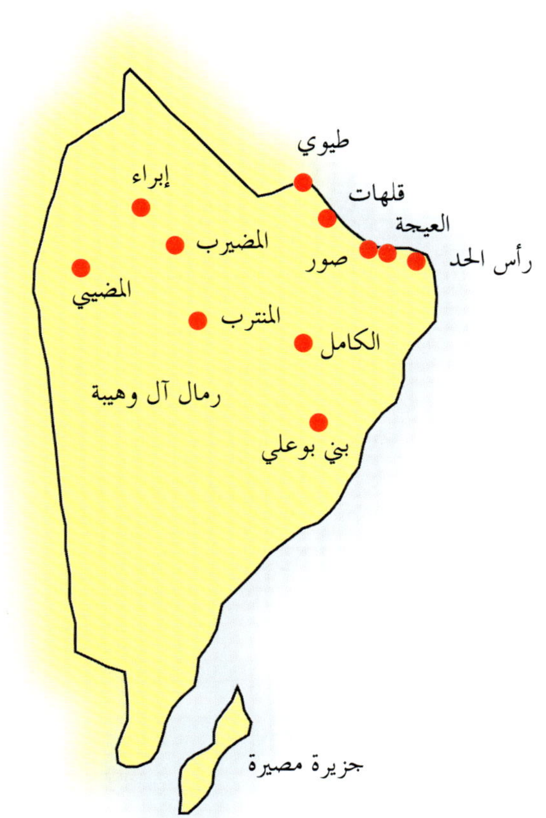

الشرقية

تقع المنطقة الشرقية شرقي وادي سمائل وتعمل كخط فاصل بين جبال الحجر الغربي والشرقي من طيوي في الشرق إلى جزيرة مصيرة في الجنوب الشرقي عبر رأس الحد. وتضم الأراضي الداخلية منه جبال الحجر الشرقي والعديد من الأودية ومنها وادي شعب ووادي طيوي ووادي الطائيين ووادي بني خالد ، ورمال آل وهيبة، وهي عبارة عن رمال بحرية قديمة إسفينية الشكل. وصور هي أهم مدينة في المنطقة الشرقية ولها شهرة تاريخية في بناء السفن التي تنطلق منها إلى أفريقيا . وتضم أهم المدن الداخلية بلاد بني بو علي والمنترب على أطراف رمال آل وهيبة والمضيرب وابراء في سهول جبال الحجر . وتقطن المنطقة الشرقية عدة قبائل لعبت دوراً بارزاً في تاريخ عمان على مر الأزمان .

Bombardment of Muscat, on the coast of Arabia, by the Sultan (1868). السلطان يقصف مسقط بالمدافع (١٨٦٨)

Tower burial tombs (c. 2000 BC) in the Eastern Hajar

القبور البرجية (٢٠٠٠ قبل الميلاد) في الحجر الشرقي

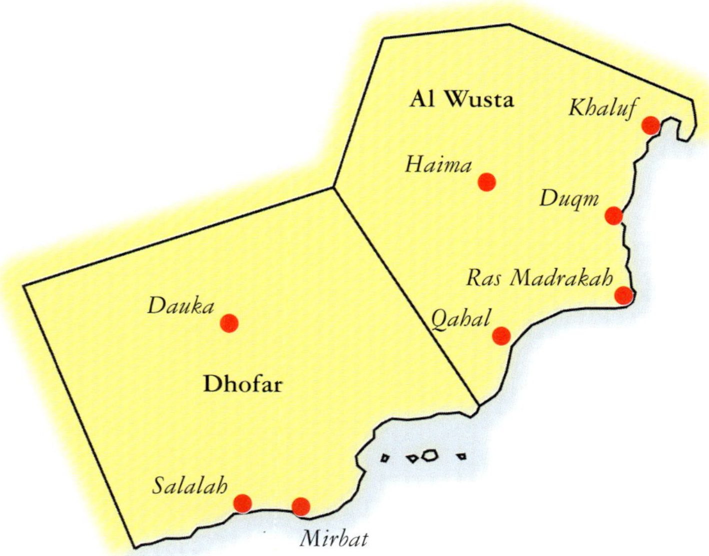

Al Wusta and Dhofar

The Al Wusta province covers the heart of the Jiddat al Harasis desert, a large area of predominantly flat gravel plains rolling in from the edge of the Empty Quarter of Saudi Arabia in the west to the Huqf area and beaches of the Arabian Gulf in the east. In the south and north it merges with the desert areas of Dhofar and Dhahira, and Dakhiliyah and Sharqiya, respectively. Al Wusta gets very little rain and is sparsely populated except for a few fishing villages along the coast and the new towns of Haima and Duqm, which were both built after the discovery of oil in the late 1970s. The Al Wusta is the homeland of the Harasis tribe, one of the largest of the Beduin tribes in Oman.

Dhofar is the southernmost province of Oman and has Salalah as its capital. This area occupies about one-third of the total area of Oman and houses about ten percent of the population. To the west and north, Dhofar shares a border with Yemen and Saudi Arabia, while in the south and east it is bounded by the Arabian Sea. The northern part of Dhofar is little more than a continuation of the Jiddat al Harasis desert. But the southern part, comprising the Qara Mountain Range and the Salalah coastal plain, receives every year between June and September the southwest monsoon rains. These rains nourish dense coconut palm groves, fruit gardens, grain fields and carpet the hills with a green lustre.

As early as 1000 BC, Dhofar gained fame as the production area of the priceless frankincense that ships and caravans carried as far north as Egypt, Syria and Rome, and eastwards to India. From 1965 to 1975, Dhofar was the terrain of a communist-led rebellion. Following the end of hostilities, Dhofar has seen rapid development on all fronts. New infrastructure, including a port at Raysut, was built and traditional economic activities, such as agricultural and fisheries, modernised.

White sand dunes on the coast near Khaluf, 1997.

كثبان رملية بيضاء على الساحل قرب خلوف، ١٩٩٧

Some of Oman's oldest rocks, exposed in the Huqf area, 1997.

صخور من بين أقدم الصخور في عمان بارزة في منطقة الحقف، ١٩٩٧

صخور بركانية سوداء ورمال ساحلية بيضاء في رأس مدركة، ١٩٩٦

Black volcanic rocks and white coral sand beaches at Ras Madrakah, 1996.

The Pink Lagoon near Qahal, 1997. The pink colour is caused by the algae that thrive in these hyper-saline waters.

بحيرة قرنفلية قرب القابل، ١٩٩٧. واكتسبت البحيرة هذا اللون بفعل الطحالب التي تزدهر في هذه المياه شديدة الملوحة.

إنزال مواد في الدقم لحملة الحفر التي
تقوم بها شركة النفط العراقية ١٩٥٤

Duqm, landing material for the IPC drilling campaign, 1954.

برج الحفر في بئر شركة النفط العراقية القديمة هيما-١، ١٩٧٠

Derrick at the old IPC well, Haima-1, 1970.

خليج الدقم عند الجزر ١٩٩٨

Duqm bay at low tide, 1998. Little remains of IPC's activities.

احتفظ ببرج الحفر في هيما-١
وأصبح الآن معلما تذكاريا، ٢٠٠٠

The Haima-1 derrick has been preserved and is now a monument, 2000.

مدينة هيما الجديدة، ٢٠٠٠

The new town of Haima, 2000.

Beduin family on the move with all their belongings, 1971.

تنقل أسرة بدوية ، ١٩٧١

Beduin gathering near Dauka, 1971.

تجمع هؤلاء البدو قرب الدوكة، ١٩٧١

Massive sand dunes near Dauka, 1971.

كثبان رملية ضخمة قرب الدوكة، ١٩٧١

Sand dunes near Dauka, 1979.

كثبان رملية ضخمة قرب الدوكة، ١٩٧٩

الخضرة والمياه الدافقة قرب عين رزات، ١٩٩٦

Green woodlands, shrubs and plenty of water near Ayn Razat, 1996.

جمال ترعى في المنحدرات الخضراء لجبل سمحان، ١٩٩٨

Camels grazing below the green slopes of the Jebel Samhan, 1998.

تستخدم حقول الحبوب والمزارع في صلالة أنظمة الري الحديثة، ٢٠٠٠

Salalah, fields of grain and gardens with modern sprinkler installation, 2000.

ساحل المغسيل، ٢٠٠٠

Mughsayl beach, 2000.

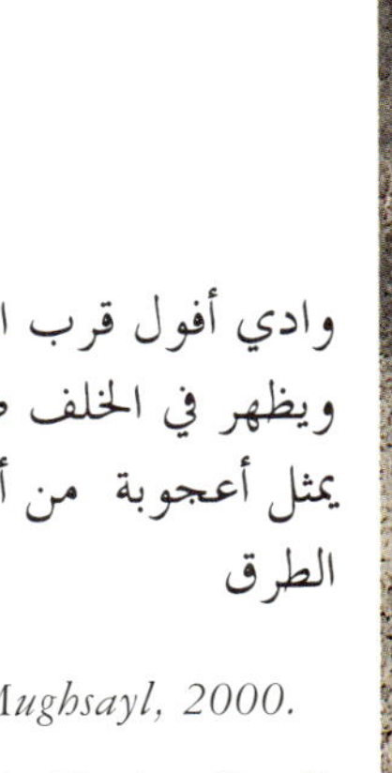

وادي أفول قرب المغسيل، ٢٠٠٠
ويظهر في الخلف طريق متعرج
يمثل أعجوبة من أعاجيب بناء
الطرق

Wadi *Afawl near Mughsayl, 2000.*
In the background, the 'Furious Road',
a miracle of road building.

SALALAH, the administrative and residential centre of Dhofar, stands at the seaward rim of a verdant fertile crescent, walled off from the desert in the interior by the Qara Mountains. Surrounded by extensive gardens, Salalah has a lush tropical appearance unlike any other town in Oman. In 1958 Sultan Said bin Taimur moved his residence from Muscat to Salalah, and the Al Hisn Royal Palace effectively became the seat of government of Oman until 1970, when Sultan Qaboos moved the government back to Muscat after taking over from his father. Since the end of the Dhofar war in 1975, Salalah has been completely modernised and expanded whilst retaining its significance as large and important marketplace.

Salalah, Al Hisn gate of the Royal Palace complex, 1972.

بوابة الحصن لمجمع القصر السلطاني في صلالة، ١٩٧٢

صلالة هي المركز الإداري والسكني في محافظة ظفار وتضم سهلا خصبا تكسوه الخضرة من ناحية البحر ومن ناحية تفصله عن الصحراء جبال قارة . وتحيط بصلالة حدائق واسعة وتتميز دون سواها من مدن السلطنة بمناخها الاستوائي ذي الخضرة الوفيرة. وكان السلطان سعيد بن تيمور قد نقل عام ١٩٥٨ ، مقر سكنه من مسقط إلى صلالة وأصبح قصر الحصن بالتالي مقرا لكرسي العرش، إلى أن تولى حضرة صاحب الجلالة السلطان قابوس بن سعيد المعظم حفظه الله ورعاه – مقاليد الحكم عام ١٩٧٠ حيث أعاد جلالته مقر الحكم إلى مسقط . ومنذ نهاية الحرب في عام ١٩٧٥ ظهرت في صلالة المرافق الحديثة وتوسعت المدينة عمرانيا وعززت من مكانتها التجارية الهامة .

Salalah, Al Hisn gate of the Royal Palace complex, 2000.

بوابة الحصن لمجمع القصر السطاني في صلالة، ٢٠٠٠

Salalah, Royal Palace, 1972.

القصر السلطاني في صلالة، ١٩٧٢

Salalah, Al Nahdah street, 1972.

شارع النهضة في صلالة، ١٩٧٢

قصر جلالة
السلطان قابوس،
٢٠٠٠

Salalah, the Palace of Sultan Qaboos, 2000.

شارع النهضة والمنتزه، ٢٠٠٠ على
اليسار بقايا بيوت بنيت بأحجار
الشعاب المرجانية.

Salalah, corner of Al Nahdah and Al Montazah streets, 2000. On the left, one of the remaining coral-stone houses.

شارع النهضة،
٢٠٠٠

Salalah, Al Nahdah street, 2000.

MIRBAT, about 65 km east of Salalah, has a natural harbour in a secluded bay. It also was an important port for the frankincense trade, but now fishing provides the revenues. In the old centre of Mirbat there are still some 19th century multi-storied merchant houses, witnesses to the lucrative trading of the past.

ميناء مرباط، ١٩٩٨

Mirbat harbour, 1998.

منزل في مرباط ونلاحظ النافذة المزينة والغنجة، ٢٠٠٠

Mirbat, detail of the house, 2000. Note the decorated window and dhow.

بيت قديم لأحد التجار في مرباط، ٢٠٠٠

Mirbat, old merchant house, 2000.

تقع مرباط شرقي صلالة بنحو ٦٥ كيلومترا وبها مرفأ طبيعي يقع في خليج منعزل. وكانت مرباط فيما مضى ميناء هاما لتصدير اللبان غير أن مهنة صيد الأسماك هي التي تمثل مصدر الدخل حاليا . وتشاهد في وسط المدينة بعض المساكن القديمة ذات الطوابق المتعددة التي تقف شاهدا على ماضيها التجاري المزدهر .

ضريح بن علي العلوي والمقبرة في مرباط، ٢٠٠٠

Bin Ali Alawi's tomb and the cemetery near Mirbat, 2000.

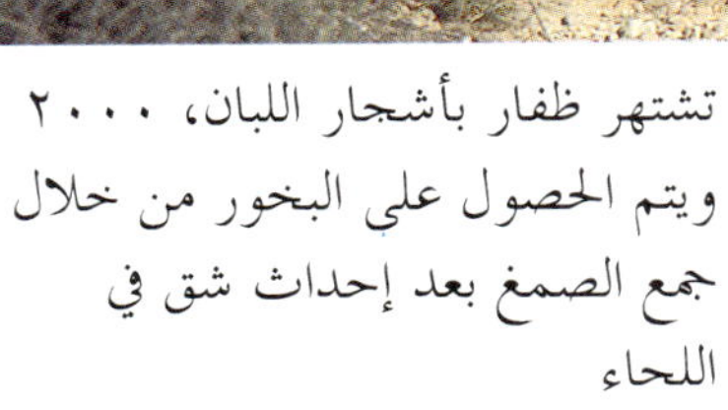

تشتهر ظفار بأشجار اللبان، ٢٠٠٠
ويتم الحصول على البخور من خلال جمع الصمغ بعد إحداث شق في اللحاء

Dhofar's famous frankincense trees, 2000. The incense is obtained by collecting the gum resin after an incision has been made in the bark.

خور روري قرب طاقة، ٢٠٠٠ على ضفاف هذا الخليج كانت سمهرم، التي غدت الآن أطلالا، بعد أن كانت في يوم من الأيام ميناءا مهما لتصدير اللبان

Khor Rawri creek near Taqah, 2000. On the banks of this creek, Sumhuram, now in ruins, was once an important port for the export of frankincense.

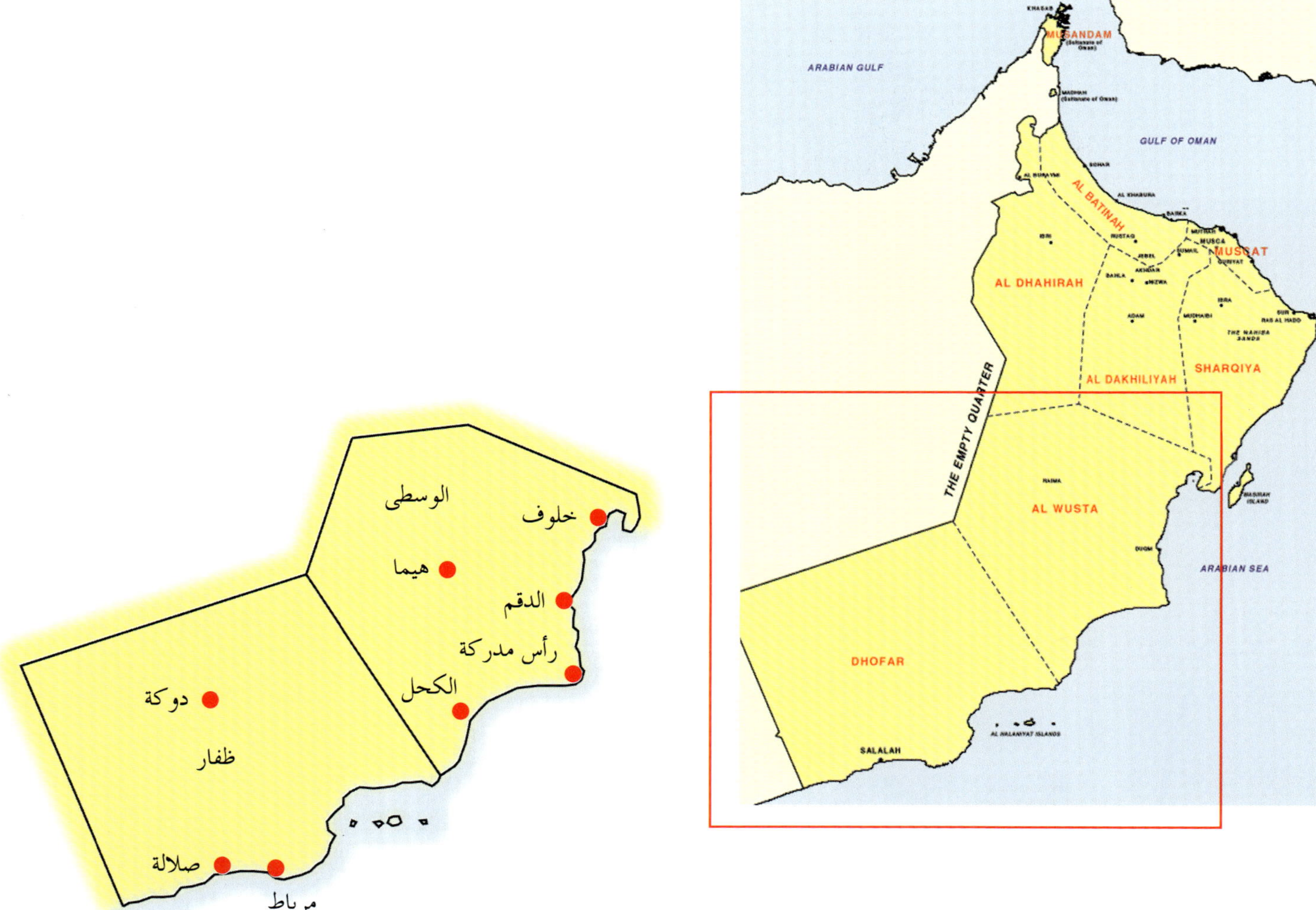

المنطقة الوسطى ومحافظة ظفار

تضم المنطقة الوسطى صحراء جدة الحراسيس وهي منطقة كبيرة تغطي معظم أجزائها سهول حصبائية منبسطة تنحدر من أطراف صحراء الربع الخالي الممتدة من المملكة العربية السعودية في الغرب إلى منطقة الحقف وشواطىء البحر العربي في الشرق . أما من ناحيتي الجنوب والشمال فهي تتاخم المناطق الصحراوية في كل من محافظة ظفار ومنطقة الظاهرة والداخلية والشرقية على التوالي . ولا تشهد المنطقة أمطارا غزيرة وهي ليست كثيفة السكان بوجه عام ما عدا في بضع قرى الصيد على الساحل وفي مدينتي هيما والدقم اللتين انشئتا بعد اكتشاف النفط في نهاية السبعينيات . وتقطن المنطقة الوسطى قبيلة الحراسيس وهي واحدة من أكبر القبائل البدوية في عمان .

تقع محافظة ظفار في الجزء الجنوبي من السلطنة وعاصمتها صلالة .وتضم مساحة محافظة ظفار نحو ثلث إجمالي مساحة السلطنة . وتبلغ نسبة سكانها نحو ١٠ في المائة من مجموع السكان وتتاخم محافظة ظفار من جهتي الغرب والشمال حدود اليمن والمملكة العربية السعودية فيما يحدها من جهتي الجنوب والشرق بحر العرب . ويعد الجزء الشمالي من المحافظة امتدادا لصحراء جدة الحراسيس . غير أن جزءها الجنوبي والذي يضم سلسلة جبال قارة وسهل صلالة الساحلي يشهد أمطارا موسمية خلال الفترة من يونيو إلى سبتمبر وتكثر فيها أشجار جوز الهند وحدائق الفواكه والحقول والمروج التي تكسو قمم الجبال.

وتشتهر محافظة ظفار منذ عهد قديم يعود إلى عام ١٠٠٠ ق . م بإنتاج اللبان الذي كانت تصدره إلى مختلف أنحاء العالم كمصر وسوريا وروما وشرقا حتى الهند. وكانت منطقة ظفار خلال الفترة من ١٩٦٥ - ١٩٧٥ معقلا لتمرد شيوعي. وشهدت المنطقة عقب انتهاء التمرد طفرة إنمائية هائلة شملت كل مناحي الحياة . فأنشئت المرافق الحديثة ومنها ميناء ريسوت وازدهرت الأنشطة الاقتصادية التقليدية كالزراعة وصيد الأسماك باستخدام المعدات الحديثة .

Sumhuram at Khor Rawri, the ancient frankincense port. سمهرم في خور روي، الميناء القديم لتصدير اللبان

Oman, detail from map Arabia (J. Blaeu 1662)

عمان، ... خارطة شبه الجزيرة العربية (جوبلو ١٦٦٢)

عمان

الماضي والحاضر

برعاية

شركة تنمية نفط عمان

حضرة صاحب الجلالة السلطان قابوس بن سعيد المعظم

تأليف: إريك فان سخربتريل

أس بي بي أكاديميك ببليكيشن،

لاهاي، هولندا

ترجمة: الزاكي عبد الحميد أحمد

آي اس بي أن ٩٠٥١٠٣١٣٩٤

ألتقطت صور شناص من ناحية البحر ومسقط من المرفأ ومرفأ مسقط من جهة صخرة الصيادين ومطرح من ناحية الشرق بعدسة آر. تمبل (١٨٠٩-١٨١٠) ونشرت بإذن من المكتبة البريطانية.

ألتقطت صور الخليج ومدينتي مسقط ومطرح بعدسة دي فان دير فلدن (١٦٩٦) ونشرت بإذن من مكتبة جامعة ليدن.

الناشر: أس بي بي أكاديميك ببليشينج ص ب ٩٧٧٤٧-٢٥٠٩ جي سي، لاهاي، هولندا
تصميم الجرافيك: سيس فان روتن، لاهاي، هولندا
الطباعة الحجرية: أوأ سيس برودكشتر، هولندا
الطباعة والتجليد: بروست أن في تروهاوت، بلجيكا

المحتويات

شكر وعرفان

أعرب عن عظيم شكري وامتناني لكل من ساهم في جعل تأليف هذا الكتاب ممكناً. لقد أبدى كل من اتصلت به، بدون استثناء، كامل استعداده في تزويدي بالأفلام الفتوغرافية والصور والمواد الأخرى لنشرها. والشكر موصول أيضاً لزوجتي كارلا على مساعدتها لي كما اشكر صهري جوريان ماستنبروك الذي شاركني في بلورة فكرة الكتاب. ولا يفوتني أن أشكر شركة تنمية نفط عمان (ش م م) على دعمها المادي واللوجستي. وأخص بالشكر الشيخ منصور بن ناصر بن علي العامري الذي زودني بالنصح والمشورة منذ بداية مشروع هذا الكتاب وحتى نهايته. واشكر أيضاً أس جيه براكاش الذي التقط بعدسته معظم صور عمان الحاضر والذي رافقني في العديد من الرحلات التي قمت بها داخل عمان.

إي. فان سخربتريل

مساهمات صور عمان الماضي
سي بالهوزين
دبليو وأم فان بسكوم
دبليو جيه فان دي بوش
آر أيه بلسترا
أن دبليو ايكهوسن
جي أم جراهام
أل دبليو فان هليموند
جيه هورستينك
جي. جيه. مستنبروك
جي أل إي فان ميربيك
إي جي جيه ميربيك
قسم الأرشيف بشركة تنمية نفط عمان
دبليو إي بيلار
إي. فان سكربتريل
دبليو أن ستينكن
أل جيه فان فين
دي فان دير ويل

مساهمات صور عمان الحاضر
سي فان سخربتريل
إي فان سخربتريل
دائرة رسم الخرائط بشركة تنمية نفط عمان
بول كونرت
جيرارد بوسمان
راشد بن علي الهنائي
دائرة العلاقات العامة بشركة تنمية نفط عمان
جي. آر. جرينويل
أس. جيه. بركاش
عبدالحميد الزاكي
صالح بن سالم العلوي

تمهيد

تبلورت فكرة هذا الكتاب،أول ما تبلورت، عقب عودتي عام ١٩٩٦ من رحلة إلى عمان. فحين قارنت الصور التي التقطتها خلال رحلتي هذه مع صور يعود تاريخها إلى أواخر الستينيات وبداية السبعينيات أيقنت بضرورة توثيق التطور الهائل الذي شهدته السلطنة منذ يوليو ١٩٧٠ توثيقاً فتوغرافياً وتضمينه في كتاب حتى يتسنى للجميع الاطلاع عليه.

وعندما بدأت في التفكير جدياً في تنفيذ مشروع الكتاب سرعان ما أدركت بأنني في حاجة لمزيد من الصور بحيث تغطي فكرة ما كان عليه الوضع في الماضي في كل أنحاء البلاد. لقد كانت هناك حينها قيود على السفر إلى بعض المناطق لاسيما مسندم وظفار وكانت مجموعتي من الصور متواضعة. لذلك اتصلت ببعض زملائي القدامى ممن عملوا في عمان قبل سنوات عدة فأمدوني بمجموعة من الصور تفوق خمسة آلاف فيلم فتوغرافي قديم كي أختار منها ما تناسبني.

على أن كمية الصور التي تفضل بها زملائي علي واجهتني بمشكلة عدم كفاية ما لدي من صور لتغطي فكرة ما عليه الوضع الآن. فمع توسع مجال فكرة الكتاب متجاوزاً حدود مواردي المتواضعة اتصلت بشركة تنمية نفط عمان ملتمساً منها المساعدة. فتفضلت مشكورة بمد يد العون لي مادياً ولوجستياً. فقمت بعدة رحلات إلى كل أنحاء البلاد لأسجل بعدستي مرة أخرى تلك الصور التي كانت في الأصل ضمن المجموعة المختارة لتغطية جوانب الماضي من الكتاب.

وتوصلت في مرحلة مبكرة إلى قرار مفاده أن الصور التي سألتقطها حديثاً ليس من الضروري أن تكون لنفس الشيء أو تصور من نفس الزاوية التي التقطت منها الصورة القديمة. وذلك إما بسبب استحالة تحقيق ذلك من الناحية العملية ذلك أننا نجد في كثير من الحالات أن ما كانت أرضاً بيضاء حينها لم تعد كذلك بفضل العمران الذي شملها وإما أن المقارنات الفتوغرافية قصد منها أن تكون بين صور مطبوعة في الذهن أكثر مما هي بين صور حقيقية يسهل فيها تحديد الفوارق إن قورنت مع بعضها البعض.

إي. فان سخربتريل

تصدير

بسم الله الرحمن الرحيم وبه نستعين

حبا الله سبحانه وتعالى عمان بجمال طبيعي يكتسب تفرده من تباين عناصره: فكأننا بالرواسي الشامخات في الشمال وهي تسمُق رُواءً بخضرة الجنوب وبالفيافي البكر في الغرب وهي تذيب صهدها في حميمية الخلجان في الشرق.

على أن عمان رغم جمالها الأخاذ لم تكن معروفة للعالم الخارجي حتى يوليو ١٩٧٠ حين تولى حضرة صاحب الجلالة السلطان قابوس بن سعيد المعظم —حفظه الله ورعاه— مقاليد الحكم في البلاد. فمنذئذ ظلت عمان تنعم بالنهضة المباركة التي أحالتها إلى دولة عصرية حديثة في ظل القيادة الرشيدة للمقام السامي.

إن قطاع النفط والغاز اسهم بقدر كبير في التطور الهائل الذي ظلت البلاد تشهده طوال العقود الثلاثة الماضية. فمعدلات الإنتاج الآخذة في الإزدياد وفرت معظم التمويل اللازم للمشروعات التنموية في الماضي والحاضر في حين يؤمّن الاحتياطي المتنامي للنفط والغاز تمويل المشروعات المستقبلية.

إن هذا الكتاب لعله يميط اللثام لأول مرة للكثير من القراء عن أن نجاح محاولات البحث عن النفط والغاز في عمان سبقته محاولات لم تخل من انتكاسات وإحباطات قبل أن يبدو الآن نجاحاً مضموناً. ويتجول الكتاب بالقاريء الكريم من خلال عيون الكاميرا ليس فقط بين أوجه التغيير الكثيرة التي شهدتها عمان منذ تولي حضرة صاحب الجلالة لزمام الحكم وإنما يعكس كذلك الثوابت الراسخة في التقاليد العمانية والحفاظ على الموارد الطبيعية.

إن مجرد إلقاء نظرة مقارنة بين صور الماضي والحاضر يجعل الألسن تلهج بالشكر والعرفان لجلالة السلطان المفدى على نهجه الحكيم الذي يؤمن الحياة الكريمة لأبناء عمان ويسمو بالبلاد عزة ورفعة.

الدكتور محمد بن حمد بن سيف الرمحي
وزير النفط والغاز

ثبت المراجع

Beguin Billecocq, Xavier, *Oman: Twenty-Five Centuries of Travel Writing,* Relations Internationales & Culture, Paris, 1994

Van Dam, N. et al., *Nederland en de Arabische wereld van de middeleeuwen tot de twintigste eeuw*, De Tijdstroom, Lochem, 1987

Dinterman, Walter, *Forts of Oman*, Motivate Publishing, 1993

Graham, Gavin, *Oman and PDO-An Introduction*, 1997

Hawley, Sir Donald, *Oman and its Renaissance*, Stacey International, London, 1990

Hill, A. and Hill, D., *The Sultanate of Oman*, Longman, London, 1977

Meyer, Pierre, *Sultanate of Oman*, Editions Delroisse, 1975

Peyton, W.D., *Old Oman*, Stacey International, 1983

Phillips, Wendell, *Oman: A History*, Librairie Du Liban, Beirut, 1971

Skeet, Ian, *Oman Before 1970: The End of an Era*, Faber & Faber, London, 1974

Oman, Department of Information, Muscat, 1972

Oman, A Seafaring Nation, Ministry of National Heritage and Culture, 1979

PDO News-4/1989,-1/1990,- 4/1995,-1,-2/1997,-1/1998

أهم الأحداث في تاريخ عمان

ظلت عمان منذ عصر قديم يعود تاريخه إلى عام ٥٠٠٠ ق . م. تلعب في أوقات مختلفة دوراً هاماً في تاريخ شبه الجزيرة العربية وما وراءها. ونورد فيما يلي بعض أهم معالم تاريخ عمان.

ما قبل التاريخ : آثار لمستوطنات ساحلية وداخلية معزولة ويرجع علماء الآثار تاريخ القبور التي اكتشفت في رأس الحمراء إلى الألف الرابع قبل الميلاد.

٣٠٠٠-٢٠٠٠ ق . م : عمان تزود دلمون (البحرين) وبلاد ما وراء النهرين ووادي الإندس بمواد أولية مختلفة منها النحاس – وظهرت في هذه الفترة المقابر المعقدة (مقابر بات بالقرب من عبري ومقابر البرج في جبال الحجر الشرقي).

٢٠٠٠-١٠٠٠ ق.م : انحسار تجارة النحاس . الفارسيون يحتلون ساحل عمان ويستوطنون فيه. وصول القبائل العربية.

١٠٠٠-٣٠٠ ق.م : ترويض الجمال، ظهور نظام الأفلاج وانتشار الزراعة بسرعة . سايروس الأعظم يفتح عمان .

٣٠٠ ق. م- ٢٢٦م : ازدهار تجارة اللبان من سمهرم في ظفار . وصول قبائل الأزد بزعامة مالك بن فهم إلى عمان ويهزمون الفرس .

٢٢٦-٦٤٠ م : الفرس يستعيدون السيطرة على ساحل الباطنة (فترة الساسانيين) . الأزديون يواصلون الحكم في الداخلية.

٦٣٠ م : عمان تعتنق الإسلام

٧٥١ م : انتخاب الجلندى بن مسعود كأول إمام .

القرن الثامن – القرن العاشر : العرب يوسعون نشاطهم التجاري والبحري بسرعة ويتخذون من صحار مركزاً لأنشطتهم البحرية .

١٢٥٠-١٥٠٧ : هرمز يؤسس دولة في ساحل عمان .

١٥٠٧-١٦٢٤ : البرتغاليون بقيادة البوكيرك يستولون على قلهات وقريات ومسقط وصحار وهرمز ويسيطرون على التجارة في المحيط الهندي. انشاء قلعتي الميراني والجلالي في مسقط .

١٦٢٤ : انتخاب ناصر بن مرشد أول إمام لليعاربة . البرتغاليون يتقهقرون إلى مطرح – مسقط .

١٦٢٤-١٧١٨ : أسرة اليعاربة تحكم عمان . طرد البرتغاليين من عمان في ١٦٥٠ . الأسطول العماني يستولي على المستعمرات البرتغالية في شرق أفريقيا والهند وفارس. بناء القلاع في نزوى وجبرين والرستاق والحزم.

١٧١٨-١٧٤٧ : اندلاع الصراعات القبلية بين قبيلتي الغافري والهناوي في أعقاب الخلاف حول الإمامة . طلب المساعدة من البرتغال ، البرتغاليون يستولون على أجزاء من عمان .

١٧٤٧ : أحمد بن سعيد يطرد البرتغاليين من عمان وينتخب أول إمام لأسرة البوسعيد .

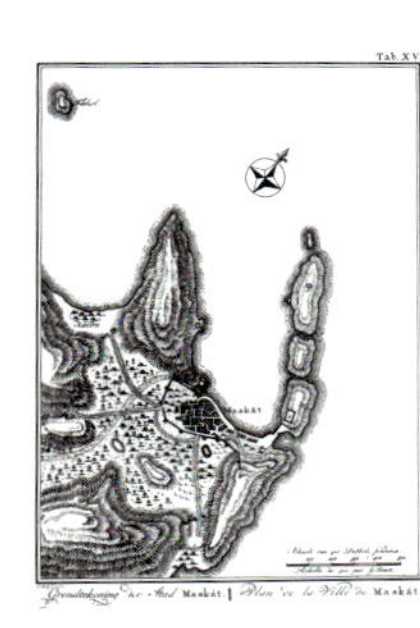

١٨٠٤-١٨٥٦ : عهد السيد سعيد بن سلطان البوسعيد . عصر ذهبي شهد الكثير من الازدهار والتوسع . انتقل كرسي الحكم من مسقط إلى زنجبار . بعد وفاة السيد سعيد انقسمت عمان وزنجبار إلى سلطنتين منفصلتين.

١٨٦٨-١٩٢٠ : انحسار مضطرد للهيمنة البحرية لعمان بسبب افتتاح قناة السويس وقدوم السفن التي تعمل بالبخار . فترة الخلافات بين السلطان الذي يحكم المناطق الساحلية والإمام الذي يسيطر على الداخلية .

١٩٢٠ : اتفاقية السيب بين السلطان والإمام بتحديد مناطق النفوذ لكل منهما .

١٩٥٢-١٩٥٥ : صراع البريمي بين المملكة العربية السعودية وأبوظبي وعمان .

١٩٥٤-١٩٥٩ : صراع الإمامة بزعامة غالب بن علي ويعرف أيضاً بحرب الجبل.

١٩٦٥-١٩٧٥ : التمرد الشيوعي في ظفار .

١٩٦٧ : بداية إنتاج النفط بكميات تجارية في عمان .

١٩٧٠ : حضرة صاحب الجلالة السلطان قابوس بن سعيد يتولى مقاليد الأمور في البلاد كحاكم ثامن من أسرة البوسعيد.

١٩٧٠ فصاعداً : النهضة العمانية . ثلاثة عقود من التنمية على نطاق واسع شملت البنية الأساسية والصحة والتعليم والمواصلات والزراعة وقطاع الأسماك والتعدين الخ والتي نقلت عمان من بلد في العصور الوسطى إلى دولة عصرية تتمتع بكل مزايا العصر وتتبوأ مكانتها بين جاراتها وبقية دول العالم.

الجمهورية الإسلامية الإرانية
خصب
بخاء
مسندم
(سلطنة عمان)
مدحا
(سلطنة عمان)
شناص
صحار
محضة
البريمي
الخابورة
السويق
السوادي
الإمارات العربية المتحدة
الحزم
الرستاق
نخل
فنجا
القرم
مطرح
مسقط
قريات
سمائل
الجبل الأخضر
المسفاة
الحمراء
بهلاء
نزوي
بركة الموز
إزكي
الحجر الشرقي
عبري
الخوير
طيوي
قلهات
صور
رأس الحد
إبراء
المضيرب
القابل
المضيبي
سناو
المنترب
أدم
الكامل
بلاد بني بوعلي
الأشخرة
وهيبة
فهود
جبال
الهويسة
أم السميم
المملكة العربية السعودية
سيح نهيدة
سيح رول
قرن علم
بارك
الربع الخالي
الحقف
جزيرة مصيرة
بهجة
هيما
الدقم
الربع الخالي
مخيزنة
رأس مدراكة
ريما
دوكة
نمر
مرمول
خليج صوقرة
جزر الحلانيات
جبال ظفار
صلالة
مرباط
الجمهورية

موجز تاريخي عن صناعة النفط والغاز في سلطنة عمان

البدايات الباكرة (١٩٠٠-١٩٢٤)

يعود الفضل في اكتشاف النفط بكميات تجارية لأول مرة في الشرق الأوسط عام ١٩٠٨، إلى ويليام نوكس دي آرسي، وهو رجل إنجليزي أثرى من التنقيب عن الذهب في أستراليا. وأصبح المشروع الذي استثمر فيه ويليام نوكس يعرف في أول عهده بالشركة الأنجلو-فارسية لتصبح فيما بعد الشركة الأنجلو-ايرانية للنفط قبل أن تصير في وقت لاحق الشركة البريطانية للنفط(بي بي). وكانت أول شركة تدخل عمان للتنقيب عن النفط وإنتاجه هي شركة دي آرسي للنفط وهي فرع من الشركة الأنجلو-فارسية.

ففي عام ١٩٢٥ نجح دي آرسي في الحصول على رخصة للتنقيب عن النفط من السلطان تيمور بن فيصل مدته عامان. وخلال فصل الشتاء التالي وصل إلى البلاد فريق من الجيولوجيين كان بينهم جورج ليز وواشنطن جراي. وتحرك ليز وجراي من بيت الفلج برفقة الكابتن إيكلس من الجيش البريطاني-الهندي على رأس كتيبة من وحدة مجندي مسقط. وسلك الفريق طريقاً بمحاذاة الشاطىء ليصلوا إلى الخابورة بعد أسبوع من بداية رحلتهم (وهي الرحلة التي لا تتعدى الساعتين بالسيارة في وقتنا الحاضر). وتابع الفريق سيره بعد ذلك عبر وادي الحواسنة إلى أن وصلوا إلى منطقة كان لا بد لهم من اجتياز واد ضيق يتراوح عرضه بين ١٠-٢٠ قدماً وتحف به جدران صخريّة يبلغ ارتفاعها ٤٠ قدماً. ولتسهيل عبور الفريق قام ليز بشد سلسلة على طرفي الوادي فوق القمم الصخرية وهي السلسلة التي لا تزال موجودة إلى يومنا هذا. وبعد أن اجتاز الفريق جبال عمان تابعوا سيرهم عبر وادي الجزي متجهين صوب صحار التي بلغوها في السابع من ديسمبر ١٩٢٦. ثم واصل الفريق عمليات المسح على ظهر مركب إلى جهة الجنوب نحو مسقط ثم عبروا جزيرة مصيرة والدقم إلى مرباط في ظفار. أنجز ليز عملاً بارعاً وما زالت الكلمات التي وصف بها جبال عمان راسخة في الأذهان وهي تجذب الإنتباه إلى كنه هذه الجبال العظيمة:

"إن هذه السلسلة الجبلية، والتي أشبه ما تكون بحزام يمتد على شكل قوس كبير يطل بطرفه الناتيء على بلاد فارس بارتفاع ٩٩٠٠ قدم فوق سطح الأرض، تعد أبرز معلم على خارطة شبه الجزيرة العربية يشد الأنظار إليه لغرابته".

وفي عام ١٩٢٧ علق رئيس بعثة آرسي التنقيبية ويدعى آرنولد ويلسون بقوله " يبدو أن الجزيرة العربية بمنأى عن أي احتمال للعثور على النفط فيها " ونتيجة لذلك لم تطلب شركة آرسي للنفط تمديداً لتصريحها و لم تشهد السنوات التي تلت ذلك نشاطاً يذكر في المنطقة.

وفي عام ١٩٣٧ قامت شركة الامتيازات النفطية المحدودة، وهي فرع من شركة نفط العراق بالتوقيع على اتفاقية خيارية مدتها ٧٥ عاماً لمنطقتي عمان وظفار تديرها شركة تنمية النفط (عمان وظفار) المحدودة التي تملك اسهمها أربع شركات بنسبة ٢٣٫٧٥ في المائة لكل منها وهي شل والشركة الأنجلو-فارسية والشركة الفرنسية للنفط (سي أف بي) (التي أضحت فيما بعد فرعاً لما تعرف اليوم بتوتال فينا إلف) وشركة الشرق الأدنى للتنمية (والتي أصبحت فرعاً لما تعرف اليوم بشركة إيكسون-موبيل). أما نسبة الخمسة في المائة الباقية فكانت من نصيب شريك خامس هو شركة بارتكس.

وقام جيولوجيو شركة نفط العراق خلال عامي ١٩٣٧-١٩٣٨ بإجراء مسح على الساحل من قاعدة لهم في دبي. وعقب ذلك خططت الشركة لإجراء مسح آخر أكبر حجماً في الداخلية خلال عامي ١٩٣٨-١٩٣٩ إلا أنه فشل في تحقيق أية نتيجة نظراً لتعرض أعضاء البعثة لنيران أسلحة الأهالي فور مغادرتهم صحار وذلك على الرغم من تأكيدات الحكومة بتوفير الأمن لهم. وفي هذه الأثناء أكتشف النفط بكميات تجارية في البحرين في عام ١٩٣٢ ثم في كل من الكويت والسعودية في عام ١٩٣٨. وأسفرت هذه الاكتشافات عن التركيز مرة أخرى على أنشطة التنقيب.

وبخلاف بعض المسوحات الجيولوجية التي تمت من الجو توقفت كل أعمال التنقيب عن النفط في عمان خلال الحرب العالمية الثانية. ولكن وفي خلال عام ١٩٤٤ تم تحويل الاتفاقيات الخيارية التي أبرمت في الماضي إلى اتفاقيات امتيازات كاملة. ونظراً للاضطرابات القبلية لم تشهد عمليات التنقيب نشاطاً يذكر بعد الحرب. وعقب القيام برحلات جيولوجية قصيرة خلال عام ١٩٤٨ أعربت الشركة عن نيتها في التخلي عن منطقة امتياز ظفار. وتمت الموافقة على ذلك في يناير ١٩٥١ ونتيجة لذلك غيرت الشركة اسمها إلى شركة تنمية نفط (عمان) المحدودة.

اللقطة رقم ١: عمليات الحفر في بئر فهود-١ عام ١٩٥٦

شمال عمان (١٩٥١ - ١٩٦٠)

وفي بداية الخمسينيات وإثر مشاهدة تكوينٍ محدّب على سطح الأرض من الجو أظهر الجيولوجيون اهتماماً متزايداً بمنطقة فهود التي رأوا أنها تشابه إلى حد كبير منطقة جبل دخان التي اكتشف فيها النفط مؤخراً في قطر.

وافق السلطان سعيد في عام ١٩٥٤ على إمكانية دخول شركة تنمية نفط (عمان) المحدودة إلى الداخلية عبر منطقة الحقف في الجنوب. فتحركت البعثة في أوائل أكتوبر من عام ١٩٥٤ ترافقها قوة عسكرية، غير أن تقدمها عبر وادي مسلم وفهود كان أبطأ مما كان متوقعاً بسبب الاضطرابات الأهلية التي كانت لا تزال مستمرة. ولكن تمكنت قوات السلطان من استعادة الأمن والنظام واستعادت بالفعل مدينتي عبري ونزوى اللتين كانتا قد وقعتا في أيدي العناصر المناوئة للحكومة.

أجرت الشركة بعد ذلك المزيد من العمل الميداني وعززت من ترسيخ أقدامها في عمان. فاستجلبت جهاز حفر من قطر قامت طائرات الشحن التابعة لقوات السلطان الجوية بنقله على أجزاء إلى فهود حيث شقّ أول طريق يربطها مع إزكي. وبدأت عملية حفر البئر فهود-١ في الثامن عشر من يناير من عام ١٩٥٦. وكانت الآمال التي عقدتها الشركة على هذه البئر كبيرة إلى درجة أنها أحضرت بالجو طاقم تصوير ليقوم بتسجيل وقائع اختبار أولِ بئر نفط في عمان. ولكن وبعد أن وصل عمق

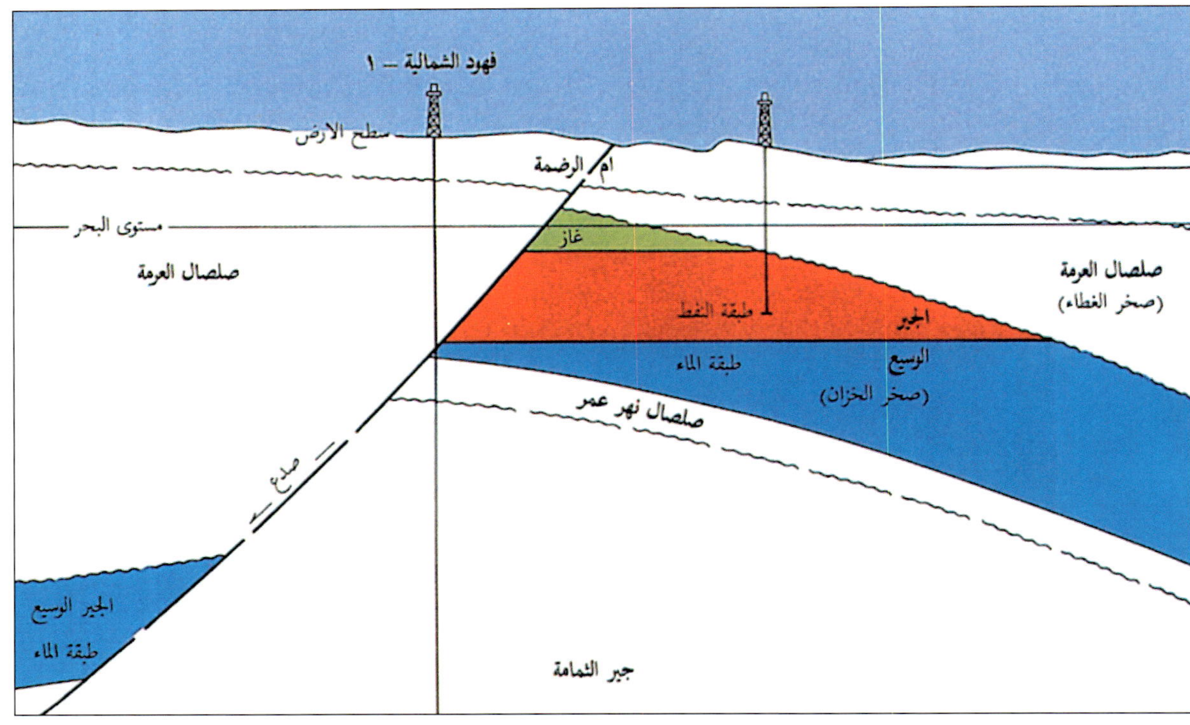

اللقطة رقم ٢: مقطع مستعرض للتراكيب الجيولوجية بفهود يظهر كيف أن البئر الأولى لم تكن تبعد سوى مسافة قصيرة عن المكمن النفطي

البئر ٣٠٠٠ مترا تخلت الشركة عن البئر في الثامن والعشرين من مايو من عام ١٩٥٧ حين أكتشف أنها بئر جافة (اللقطة رقم – ١). ولكن ما لم يدر بخلد أحد حينها هو أن هذه البئر المهجورة كانت على مرمى حجر من حقل يبلغ مخزونه النفطي عدة بلايين من البراميل إذ كان يفصل بينها وبين هذا المخزون الهائل بضع مئات من الأمتار ليس إلا (اللقطة رقم ٢). فلا غرو إذن إن وصفت بئر فهود –١ بأنها أتعس بئر في تاريخ النفط في الشرق الأوسط.

وفي هذه الأثناء قامت الشركة أيضاً خلال عام ١٩٥٧ بنقل مقرها من الدقم إلى العذيبة على ساحل الباطنة. وعرقلت الاضطرابات المستمرة أنشطة الشركة ذلك أن فجوة سمائل في وسط الجبال كانت تزرع بالألغام من وقت لآخر. ومع ذلك تمكنت الشركة من حفر بئرين استكشافيتين أثناء حرب الجبل وهما غابة–١ التي حفرت في ١٩٥٩ وهيما–١ التي حفرت بعدها بعام. وحين ثبت أن البئرين جافتان تماماً حفرت الشركة في وقت لاحق من عام ١٩٦٠ بئر عفار–١ وهي بئر ضحلة نسبياً ولكن ثبت أنها هي الأخرى محبطة كسابقتيها.

وبعد أن تجاوزت مصروفاتها ١٢ مليون دولار أمريكي دون أن تحقق نجاحاً ومع تزايد مصروفاتها الإضافية والمشاكل اللوجستية المتصلة بأجهزة الحفر الجديدة والمسوحات الزلزالية والتحريات بقياس الجاذبية قررت شركة نفط العراق أن تتخلى عن منطقة امتيازها في عمان. إلا أن شركتي شل وبارتكس فضلتا الاستمرار في حين انسحب شركاؤهما الباقون وهم الشركة الفرنسية (سي أف بي) والشركة البريطانية (بي بي) اللتان خلفتا الشركة الأنجلو–فارسية وشركة الشرق الأدنى للتنمية.

الأنشطة في ظفار (١٩٥١–١٩٦٦)

بعد أن تم التخلي عن منطقة امتياز ظفار في يناير ١٩٥١ قام السلطان سعيد بمنحها لويندل فيليبس وهو عالم آثار أمريكي كان قد قام بحفريات أثرية بالقرب من صحار. ثم عمل بعد ذلك في ظفار حيث اكتشف بقايا مدينة سمهرم وهي ميناء قديم اقترن اسمه بتجارة اللبان.

وتمكن فيليبس فيما بعد من استئجار منطقة الامتياز لشركة تأسست حديثاً تعرف باسم ظفار–سيتيز سيرفيس بتروليوم كوربوريشن وهي شركة كانت سيتيز سيرفيس وريتشفيلد كوربوريشن أوف كليفورنيا تمتلك نسبة ٥٠ في المائة من أسهمها فيما احتفظ فيليبس بإتاوة إضافية بنسبة ٢ر٥ في المائة من خلال شركته فيليبريور.

اللقطة رقم ٣: لوحة تذكارية نصبتها شركة ظفار سيتيز سيرفس عقب اكتشاف النفط في مرمول عام ١٩٥٦. واعتقد في البداية أن هذا الاكتشاف غير مجد اقتصادياً.

اللقطة رقم ٤: بدء عمليات الحفر في البئر جبال-١ بحضور والي عبري عام ١٩٦٢

بدأت أنشطة التنقيب في عام ١٩٥٣ وبعد حفر ثلاث آبار مخيبة للآمال أكتشف حقل مرمول المحدودب عام ١٩٥٧ وهو عبارة عن تكوين تقليدي منحدر في جهتين، وذلك قبل خمس سنوات من تحقيق الاكتشافات المشهورة في شمال عمان (اللقطة رقم-٣). على أن الحفر التقييمي الذي أجري فيما بعد لم يحقق معدلات إنتاج ثابت. وبنهاية عام ١٩٦١ كانت شركة ظفار-سيتيز سيرفيس بتروليوم كوربوريشن قد حفرت ٢٣ بئراً منها ست آبار تجاوزت أعماقها ٣٠٠٠ متراً، وأنفقت زهاء ٣٥ مليون دولار أمريكي. ونتيجة لذلك انسحبت شركة ريتشفيلد من المشروع. (ومن المفارقات أن عمليات التقييم التي أجريت لاحقاً في أواخر عام ١٩٧٠ أظهرت أن حقل مرمول هو أحد أكبر حقول النفط في عمان).

وفي عام ١٩٦٢ أبرمت سيتيز سيرفيس اتفاقية مع شركة جون ميكوم وهي إحدى أكبر الشركات المستقلة في تكساس وشركة بيور أويل فيما احتفظت فيليبريور بالاتاوة الاضافية البالغة نسبتها ٥ر٢ في المائة. وبحلول عام ١٩٦٥ كانت شركتا ميكوم وبيور أويل قد حفرتا خمس آبار إضافية كانت هي الأخرى نتائجها مخيبة للآمال. وفي هذه الأثناء دخلت شركة كونتننتال أويل اتفاقية امتياز ظفار كمساهم بنسبة الثلث فيما إحتفظت ميكوم بثلث في حين حصلت يونيون أويل كومباني أوف كليفورنيا على أسهم شركة بيور أويل. وحفرت بئر واحدة هي بئر المنتصر-١ التي تقع في طرف الربع الخالي في عام ١٩٦٦ وجاءت نتائجها سلبية. وبسبب الاضطرابات الأهلية في ظفار إلى جانب الفشل في تحقيق أي نجاح تخلت شركة كونتننتال وشركاؤها عن اتفاقية امتياز ظفار.

اكتشاف النفط بكميات تجارية في عمان (١٩٦١-١٩٦٩)

بعد انسحاب ثلاثة من الشركاء الخمسة الأساسيين قسمت أسهم شركة تنمية نفط (عمان) بنسبة ٨٥ في المائة لشل و١٥ في المائة لبارتكس. ولم تجر أية عمليات حفر حتى عام ١٩٦٢ حيث أكدت المسوحات الزلزالية احتمالات التركيب الجيولوجي الذي كانت المسوحات لقياس الجاذبية قد حددته أولاً في جبال. غير أن بئر جبال ١ التي بدأ حفرها في الثامن والعشرين من مايو ١٩٦٢ (اللقطة رقم-٤) واجهت مشاكل فنية. لذلك تم تحريك جهاز الحفر إلى القرب من هذه البئر للنظر في إمكانية حفر بئر أخرى فبدأ حفر بئر جبال-٢ في يونيو ١٩٦٢. ولكن لسوء الطالع عندما وصلت عمليات الحفر إلى تكوين نتيه ظهرت كميات كبيرة من الغاز وأدت إلى انفجار البئر. ومن محاسن الصدف أن أحداً لم يصب بأذى. ثم استؤنفت عمليات الحفر وفي الحادي عشر من سبتمبر ١٩٦٢ عثر على

اللقطتان رقم ٥ و٦: إنشاء خط الأنابيب الرئيسي من فهود إلى سيح المالح (ميناء الفحل) في عام ١٩٦٦

اللقطة رقم ٧: أعلى نقطة في خط الأنابيب الرئيسي في وادي سمائل (٦٥٠ مترا)

اللقطة رقم ٨: إنشاء ساحة الصهاريج الرئيسية لخام النفط في سيح المالح (ميناء الفحل)

نفط خفيف في تكوين شعيبة. وفي الخامس من أبريل من عام ١٩٦٣ تم تحريك جهاز الحفر إلى منطقة نتيه لاختبار قبو سطحي يشابه قبو فهود ولكنه أصغر منه حجماً. أثبتت البئر نتيه-١ نجاحها فسرعان ما تبعتها نتيه-٢ ونتيه-٣. وألقت المعلومات الاستراتجرافية التي تم الحصول عليها من آبار جبال و نتيه ضوءاً جديداً على النتائج التي أسفرت عنها بئر فهود-١ قبل سبعة أعوام، مما شجع الشركة على المحاولة مرة أخرى في فهود.

فبدأت عملية حفر بئر فهود-٢ في الخامس من فبراير ١٩٦٤. وأثبتت هذه البئر الجديدة والتي تقع على بعد ١٥٠٠ متراً من البئر الأولى أن تكوين نتيه بكامله تكوين حامل للنفط وأعتبرت بالتالي اكتشافاً كبيراً. وبعد تسرب هذا النبأ إلى الصحافة نشرت صحيفة صنداي تايمز اللندنية في عددها الصادر في السادس والعشرين من يوليو ١٩٦٤ مقالاً تناولت فيه النجاحات النفطية التي تحققت في عمان وأعقب ذلك تصريح رسمي صدر في الثاني

اللقطة رقم ٩: تحميل الناقلة موسبرينس بالشحنة الأولى من النفط العماني عام ١٩٦٧

من نوفمبر ١٩٦٤ عن اكتشاف كميات تجارية من النفط.

بدأ الآن الاستثمار في إنشاء خط أنابيب يمتد إلى الساحل وشراء المواد الأخرى اللازمة لنقل خام النفط العماني وتصديره ووضعت الخطط لتصدير الشحنة الأولى. وبالإضافة إلى ذلك استمرت عمليات التنقيب بروح جديدة مفعمة بالثقة والحماس.

وتسارعت عمليات تطوير الحقول ومرافق الإنتاج في فهود بما في ذلك محطة كهرباء بطاقة ٢٠ ميجاواط. كما أعدت الخطط لإنشاء مرافق المعالجة والتخزين والشحن في سيح المالح (ميناء الفحل فيما بعد) في الساحل. وستربط مناطق الإنتاج مع الساحل بخط أنابيب يبلغ في طوله ٢٧٦ كيلومتراً ويبلغ أقصى ارتفاع له في النقطة العليا في إزكي حيث يرتفع عن سطح الأرض بمقدار ٦٥٠ متراً. لقد كان مشروعاً فيه الكثير من التحدي والتعقيدات السياسية.

بدأ العمل في مارس ١٩٦٦ ولإكمال خط الأنابيب تم استيراد ما مجموعه ٦٠ ألف طن من الفولاذ ثم نقلت فشيدت في النهاية مع مرافق الضخ المرتبطة بها والمعدات الأخرى ووفرت القرى المجاورة الأيدي العاملة المطلوبة لذلك (اللقطات ٥،٦،٧،٨).
لقد بلغت الكلفة الإجمالية للمشروع بكامله بما في ذلك إنشاء مجموعة من محطات ترديد البث اللاسلكي ومساكن الموظفين في رأس الحمراء والمنطقة الصناعية وساحة الصهاريج في سيح المالح وإنشاء خط الأنابيب إلى الساحل، سبعين مليون دولار أمريكي.

وتم تصدير الشحنة الأولى من النفط العماني في السابع والعشرين من يوليو ١٩٦٧. وتم تحميل هذه الشحنة على ظهر الناقلة موسبرينس في سيح المالح وتوضح النسخة الأصلية من إشعار المدين الصادر عنها بأن الشحنة بلغت ٥٤٣٨٠٠ برميل من خام النفط العماني بيعت بمعدل ١٫٤٢ دولار للبرميل الواحد (اللقطتان ٩ و ١٠).

ودخلت عمان عصراً جديداً مع تصدير أول شحنة من خام النفط. وفي أعقاب هذه النجاحات التنقيبية، أجريت دراسات جيولوجية مكثفة على جبال عمان بما في ذلك مسحان ميدانيان كبريان خلال الفترة ١٩٦٦-١٩٦٩ تحت إشراف كيه.دبليو. جليني. وأسهمت هذه الدراسات بقدر كبير في الفهم السائد حالياً للتاريخ الجيولوجي لجبال عمان. ومن المثير للاهتمام أن نلحظ أن النتائج التي توصلت إليها هذه الدراسات أكدت في جوهرها العمل الذي سبق أن أنجزه ليز قبل أربعين عاماً.

في هذه الأثناء انضمت شركة النفط الفرنسية (سي أف بي) مرة أخرى إلى شراكة شركة تنمية نفط (عمان) من خلال حصولها

اللقطة رقم ١٠: ثلاث طوابع تذكارية بمناسبة تصدير الشحنة الأولى من النفط عام ١٩٦٧

اللقطة رقم ١١: الزيارة الأولى التي تفضل بها حضرة صاحب الجلالة السلطان قابوس بن سعيد المعظم – حفظه الله لمكاتب شركة تنمية نفط عمان في ١٨ أغسطس ١٩٧٠

اللقطة رقم ١٢: حضرة صاحب الجلالة السلطان قابوس بن سعيد المعظم – حفظه الله يستعرض حرس الشرف من شرطة المنشآت النفطية أثناء زيارته

على ١٠ في المائة من أسهم بارتكس البالغة ١٥ في المائة من أسهم الشركة مما أسفر عن توزيع أسهم الشركة على النحو التالي: شل ٨٥ في المائة وشركة النفط الفرنسية ١٠ في المائة وبارتكس ٥ في المائة. وفي عام ١٩٦٩ استعادت الشركة امتياز ظفار بموجب اتفاقية مماثلة من حيث شروطها للاتفاقية المعدلة التي أبرمت في شمال البلاد عام ١٩٦٧. وبحلول عام ١٩٧٤ كانت اتفاقية ظفار قد أدمجت بالكامل في اتفاقية الامتياز الرئيسية.

توسع الصناعة النفطية (١٩٧٠–٢٠٠٠)

في الثالث والعشرين من يوليو ١٩٧٠ تسلّم حضرة صاحب الجلالة السلطان قابوس بن سعيد المعظم، مقاليد الحكم من والده. وقام بأول زيارة له لشركة تنمية نفط عمان في الثامن عشر من أغسطس ١٩٧٠ (اللقطتان ١١ و١٢). وفي هذه الأثناء تم تشغيل صهريج تخزين خام النفط الذي تم إنشاؤه مؤخراً بسعة ٩٠٠ ألف برميل حيث تسنى بموجبه ضخ خام النفط بمعدل ٥٦ ألف برميل في الساعة في الناقلات الراسية في الميناء. وزادت خلال عام ١٩٧٠ أيضاً حصة السلطنة من الأرباح من ٥٠ في المائة إلى ٥٥ في المائة.

إن تاريخ التنقيب في عمان يضم عدة جوانب مثيرة للإهتمام منها إستدامة الاحتياطيات النفطية. فحينما تظهر علامات الاضمحلال على حقل من الحقول سرعان ما يتم التوصل إلى حقل جديد أو تمنح الحقول القائمة فرصة أخرى للإنتاج وذلك من خلال الابتكار واستخدام التكنولوجيا وموهبة الحس المهني. إن الإعتقاد السائد حين عثر على خام النفط الثقيل لأول مرة في تكوين الحوشي في حقل مرمول، كان هو أن إنتاجه غير مجد من الناحية الإقتصادية. وفي عام ١٩٧٢ أثبت اكتشاف غابة الشمالي بشكل قاطع الطبيعة التجارية الحقيقية لمثل هذه الحقول ذات النفط الثقيل. وتواصلت الاكتشافات الناجحة في التكوين حيث تمت اكتشافات هامة في سيح نهيدة وسيح رول في عامي ١٩٧٢ و١٩٧٣ على التوالي. وتقع هذه الحقول بالإضافة إلى حقلي قرن علم وحابور اللذين اكتشفا خلال عامي ١٩٧١–١٩٧٢، كلها في منطقة غابة (اللقطة ١٣). وربطت كل الحقول الخمسة الجديدة بخط الإنتاج في عام ١٩٧٥ مع تفريغ النفط من خلال أنبوب بقطر ٢٠ بوصة يربط مع خط الأنابيب الرئيسي على بعد ٧٥ كيلومتراً من فهود. ونتيجة لذلك ارتفع الإنتاج إلى ٣٤٠ ألف برميل في اليوم.

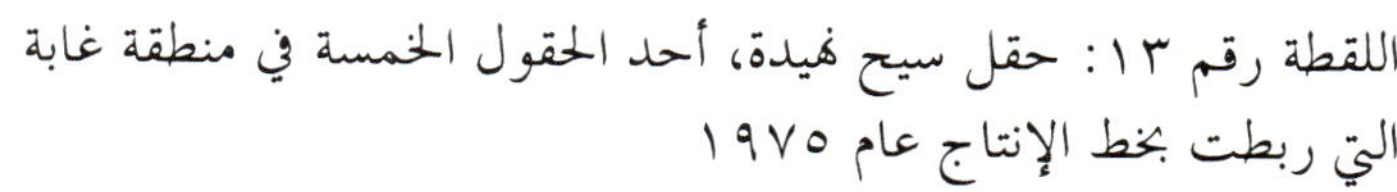

اللقطة رقم ١٣: حقل سيح نهيدة، أحد الحقول الخمسة في منطقة غابة التي ربطت بخط الإنتاج عام ١٩٧٥

في الأول من يناير من عام ١٩٧٤ حصلت حكومة السلطنة على نسبة ٢٥ في المائة من أسهم شركة تنمية نفط عمان لترتفع النسبة في يوليو من عام ١٩٧٤ بأثر رجعي يعود إلى الأول من يناير ١٩٧٤ إلى ٦٠ في المائة (اللقطة ١٤). ونتيجة لذلك أصبحت الآن أسهم الشركات المساهمة بالنسب التالية: شل (٣٤ في المائة)، توتال (٤ في المائة) وبارتكس (٢ في المائة).

أسفر ارتفاع الأسعار خلال عام ١٩٧٣ عن تحسين اقتصاديات النفط في جنوب عمان إلى حد كبير وشهدت السبعينيات نتيجة لذلك انتقال نشاط التنقيب المكثف إلى الجانب الشرقي من الحوض الملحي بجنوب عمان .وأسفرت الحملة التنقيبية الأولى عن اكتشاف حقلي أمل وأمين إلى جانب اكتشافات أخرى.

اللقطة رقم ١٤: حضرة صاحب الجلالة السلطان قابوس بن سعيد المعظم — حفظه الله أثناء توقيعه على اتفاقية المشاركة التي حصلت بموجبها الحكومة على نسبة ٢٥ في المائة من أسهم الشركة في ١ يناير ١٩٧٤ (في شهر يوليو من العام نفسه ازدادت النسبة إلى ٦٠ في المائة)

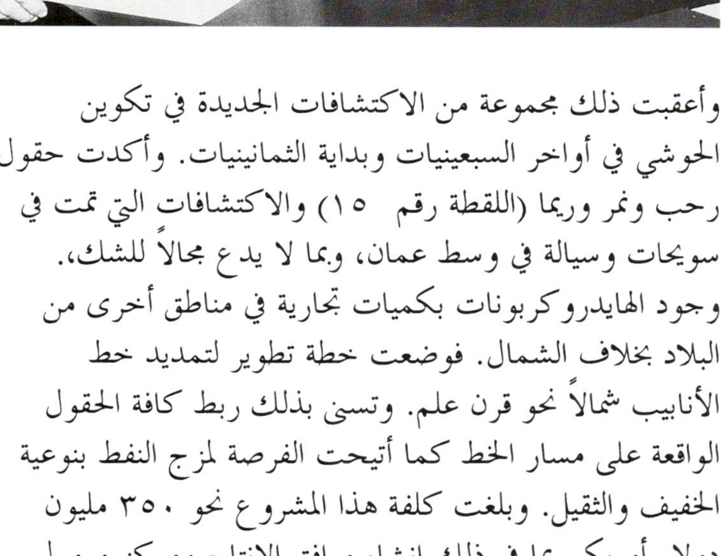

وأعقبت ذلك مجموعة من الاكتشافات الجديدة في تكوين الحوشي في أواخر السبعينيات وبداية الثمانينيات. وأكدت حقول رحب ونمر وريما (اللقطة رقم ١٥) والاكتشافات التي تمت في سويحات وسيالة في وسط عمان، وبما لا يدع مجالاً للشك، وجود الهايدروكربونات بكميات تجارية في مناطق أخرى من البلاد بخلاف الشمال. فوضعت خطة تطوير لتمديد خط الأنابيب شمالاً نحو قرن علم. وتسنى بذلك ربط كافة الحقول الواقعة على مسار الخط كما أتيحت الفرصة لمزج النفط بنوعية الخفيف والثقيل. وبلغت كلفة هذا المشروع نحو ٣٥٠ مليون دولار أمريكي بما في ذلك إنشاء مرافق الإنتاج ومركز مرمول.

وفي الخامس عشر من نوفمبر ١٩٨٠ وفي إطار احتفالات البلاد بالذكري العاشرة للعيد الوطني المجيد بدأ الإنتاج في الجنوب (اللقطة ١٨). وكانت شركة تنمية نفط عمان قد أنشئت بموجب مرسوم سلطاني كشركة محدودة المسؤولية في يناير ١٩٨٠. وفي عام ١٩٨١ كانت الشركة تنتج ٣٢٠ ألف برميل منها ٥٠ ألف برميل من الجنوب. وفي عام ١٩٨٢ افتتحت في ميناء الفحل مصفاة تبلغ طاقتها ٥٠ ألف برميل للوفاء بالمتطلبات المحلية من المنتجات النفطية. ومنذ بداية الثمانينيات ظل إجمالي إنتاج الشركة في تزايد مضطرد. فمن ٥٠٠ ألف برميل في اليوم عام ١٩٨٥ ازداد إنتاجها إلى ٦٠٠ ألف عام ١٩٨٨ ثم إلى ٨٠٠ ألف برميل في اليوم عام ١٩٩٥ وإلى نحو ٨٣٥ ألف برميل في اليوم عام ١٩٩٩ منها حوالي النصف من الجنوب.

اللقطة رقم ١٥: مركز ريما بجنوب عمان والذي افتتح عام ١٩٨٢

اللقطتان رقم ١٦ و١٧: حقل مرمول الذي بدأ في الإنتاج عام ١٩٨٢

وتعزى هذه الزيادة في جانب منها إلى رغبة الشركة في استخدام آخر ما توصلت إليه التقنية من أجل استخلاص المزيد من النفط من الحقول القائمة. وتشمل هذه الأساليب التقنية فيما تشمل الحقن بالبخار (لتخفيف النفط الثقيل ليتدفق بسهولة أكثر) والآبار الأفقية والآبار متعددة الأطراف (لجمع النفط المتدفق في ثنايا الصخور بطريقة أكثر كفاءةً) ورسم نماذج للمكامن بواسطة الكمبيوتر لمعرفة تحرك النفط في باطن الأرض بدقة أكثر.

ويعزى الجانب الآخر من الزيادة التي ظلت الشركة تحققها عبر السنوات في معدلات إنتاجها، إلى "النفط الجديد" من الحقول التي عثرت عليها وطورتها الشركة بسرعة متناهية. فخلال الفترة بين ١٩٦٧ ١٩٨٠ كان كل إنتاج الشركة من النفط يأتي من ١١ حقلاً وبحلول عام ١٩٨٨ كان إجمالي إنتاجها من النفط يأتي من ٥٠ حقلاً ليرتفع إلى ٦٠ حقلاً بحلول عام ١٩٩٠ فإلى نحو ١٠٠ حقل في عام ١٩٩٩ (شكل ٢٣) بما فيها حقل مخيزنة ذو النفط الثقيل.

إن الشركة من أجل تحقيق هدفها الطموح ذي الشقين المتمثلين في زيادة معدل إنتاجها إلى مليون برميل في اليوم بحلول عام ٢٠٠٥ مع القيام في نفس الوقت برفع احتياطيها، فلا بد لها من الاعتماد على تحقيق نجاح متواصل في جهودها التنقيبية والهندسية. وفي عالم يمكن أن تتدهور فيه أسعار النفط على حين غرة فعلى الشركة أن تراقب نفقاتها بعناية.

عمليات تطوير الغاز (١٩٧٨-٢٠٠٠)

مع أن اتفاقية امتياز الشركة كانت تغطي فقط تطوير وإنتاج النفط وأية كميات من الغاز المصاحب إلا أن الشركة أنشأت عام ١٩٧٨ بالنيابة عن الحكومة خط أنابيب للغاز بقطر ٢٠ بوصة وطوله ٣٤٥ كيلومتر، وذلك لنقل الغاز المصاحب من حقل جبال إلى الغبرة في الساحل حيث يستخدم في توليد الكهرباء ولتوفير الوقود لمحطة جديدة لتحلية المياه (اللقطتان ١٩ و٢٠). وفي عام ١٩٨١ تم تمديد خط الغاز بطول ٢٣٠ كيلومتر على طول ساحل الباطنة إلى صحار عبر أنبوب بقطر ١٦ بوصة وذلك لتوفير الطاقة لعمليات تعدين النحاس. وفي نفس الوقت أنشئت محطات لاستخلاص السوائل من الغاز المصاحب في جبال وفهود وسيح رول حيث يتم تحويل الغاز إلى منتج يمكن بيعه والذي لولا ذلك لتم التخلص منه بحرقه. وبالإضافة لذلك افتتحت محطة أخرى في جبال لإنتاج غاز البروبين (لاستخدامه في أنظمة التبريد في الشركة) وغاز البيوتان (لمصنع تعبئة الغاز في أسطوانات في الرسيل).

في عام ١٩٨٤ أبرمت اتفاقية أخرى تقوم الشركة بموجبها بالبحث عن الغاز بالنيابة عن الحكومة. وكان القصد من هذه الاتفاقية هو النظر في إمكانية تصدير الغاز إذا تحققت زيادة كبيرة في الاحتياطي ليصبح رافداً لتعزيز الاقتصاد الوطني بجانب النفط. وسرعان ما اثبتت هذه السياسة نجاحاً كبيراً إذ تم اكتشاف كميات كبيرة من الغاز في رمال مجموعة الهيما العميقة وبخاصة في سيح نهيدة وسيح رول وبارك في حوض غابة الملحي. وفي بداية التسعينيات تضاعفت كمية احتياطي الغاز غير المصاحب ثلاث مرات بحيث تكفي لتلبية الطلب المتوقع للاستهلاك المحلي مع توفير كميات كافية لمشروع تصدير الغاز الطبيعي المسال.
ويعد مشروع الغاز الطبيعي في عمان هو أكبر مشروع فردي بكل المقاييس يتم إنشاؤه في البلاد وتستثمر فيه مبالغ ضخمة في شقه العلوي أي العثور على الغاز وإنتاجه ونقله وشقه السفلي أي معالجته وإسالته وتصديره. ولقد قامت شركة تنمية نفط عمان خلال الربع الأخير من عام ١٩٩٩، بتشغيل الشق العلوي من المشروع بما في ذلك تطوير حقول الغاز ومحطة المعالجة في سيح رول وإنشاء خط الأنابيب إلى مصنع الشركة العمانية للغاز

اللقطة رقم ١٨: معالي سعيد بن أحمد الشنفري، يفتتح حقول النفط الجنوبية في نوفمبر ١٩٨٠

الطبيعي المسال (اللقطتان ٢١ و٢٢). وتم تصدير الشحنة الأولى من الغاز الطبيعي المسال في أبريل من عام ٢٠٠٠ إلى كوريا وهي أكبر مستورد للغاز الطبيعي المسال من عمان.

الآثار الاقتصادية المترتبة على اكتشاف النفط:

لقد كان لاكتشاف النفط في الشرق الأوسط آثار كبيرة على اقتصاد جميع دول المنطقة وأساليب الحياة فيها ولم تكن عمان بمستثناة. وقد أسهمت عائدات النفط بقدر كبير في تمويل المشاريع الإنمائية الهائلة التي ظلت تشهدها السلطنة على كافة الأصعدة منذ عام ١٩٧٠. إن دخل السلطنة من النفط يتكون من حصة الحكومة البالغة نسبتها ٦٠٪ من أسهم الشركة ومن الضرائب والإتاوات المفروضة على الشركات المساهمة بنسبة ٤٠٪. وبمعدل الإنتاج المستهدف البالغ ٨٥٠ ألف برميل يومياً اعتباراً من عام ٢٠٠٠ فإن قطاع النفط يسهم بنسبة كبيرة في الدخل القومي للبلاد. إن مخزون الهايدروكربون في السلطنة متواضع إذا ما قورن مع الدول الأخرى في المنطقة. لذلك كان تنويع مصادر الدخل ولا يزال عنصراً هاماً في التخطيط الاقتصادي. وسيكون مشروع الغاز الطبيعي المسال الذي نتج عن البرنامج الحكومي الطموح للتنقيب عن الغاز رافداً رئيسياً جديداً للدخل القومي.

اللقطة رقم ١٩: حضرة صاحب الجلالة السلطان قابوس بن سعيد المعظم يفتتح محطة الغاز في جبال عام ١٩٧٨

اللقطة رقم ٢٠: منظر عام لمحطة الغاز في جبال

اللقطة رقم ٢١: بمناسبة الافتتاح الرسمي لمحطة الغاز في سيح رول قدمت هدية تذكارية لصاحب السمو السيد ثويني بن شهاب، الممثل الشخصي لصاحب الجلالة (ديسمبر ١٩٩٩)

اللقطة رقم ٢٢: محطة الغاز الطبيعي المسال بعمان في ولاية صور

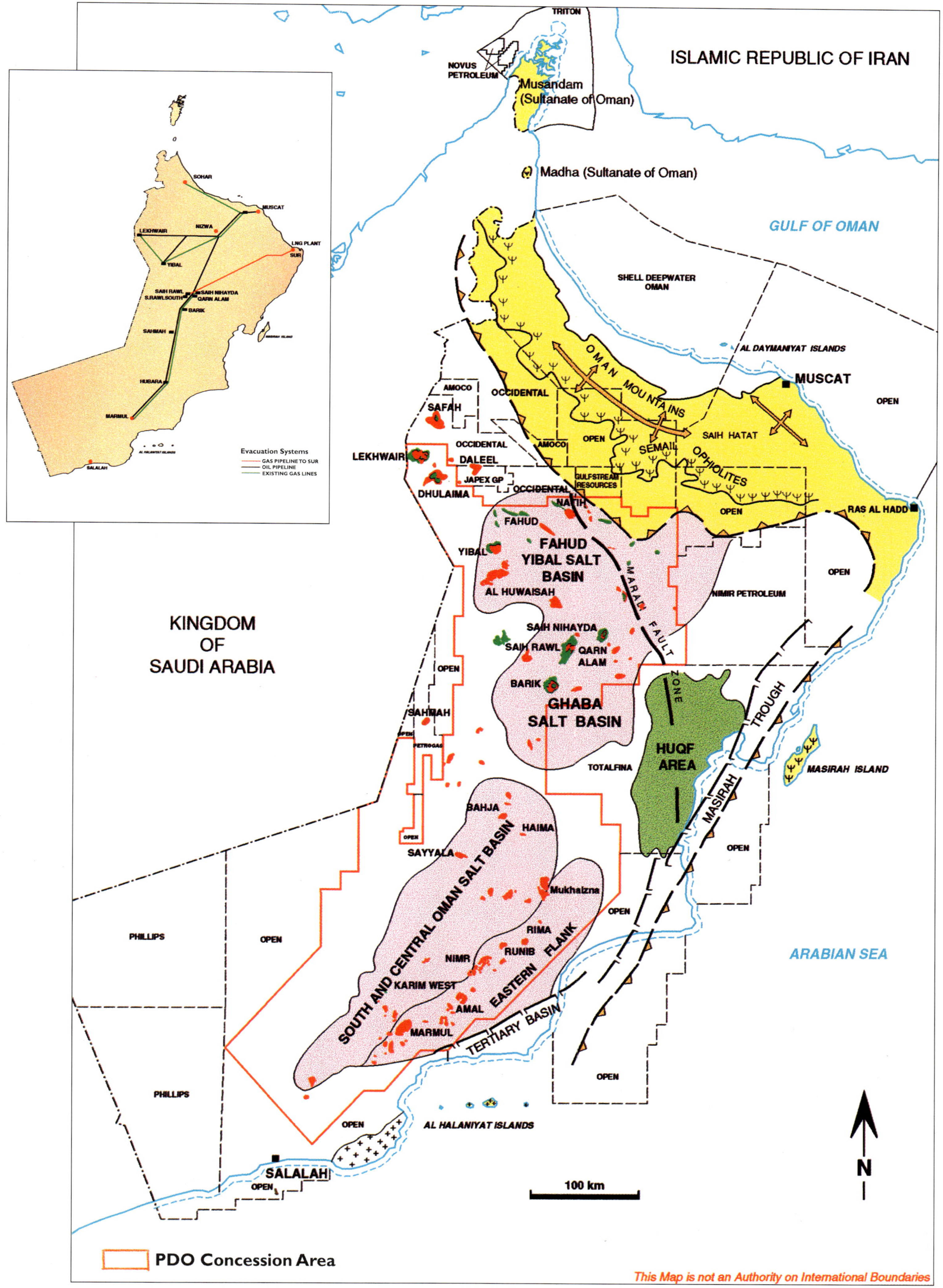

شكل ٢٣ أ و ب: أماكن تواجد النفط والغاز وأنظمة التفريغ في عمان